Catholic Identity
in Our Colleges
and Universities

Catholic Identity in Our Colleges and Universities

A Collection of Defining Documents

COMMITTEE ON EDUCATION
BISHOPS' AND PRESIDENTS' SUBCOMMITTEE
UNITED STATES CONFERENCE OF CATHOLIC BISHOPS

United States Conference of Catholic Bishops
Washington, D.C.

At its May 2005 meeting, the Bishops' Committee on Education discussed and approved the re-publication of the Catholic documents contained herein. The sources of these documents vary: five are from the Holy See and the remaining documents are from the United States Conference of Catholic Bishops (USCCB). This collection has been reviewed by Bishop Bernard J. Harrington, chairman of the committee, and approved for publication by the undersigned.

Msgr. David Malloy
General Secretary, USCCB

In 2001 the National Conference of Catholic Bishops and United States Catholic Conference became the United States Conference of Catholic Bishops.

Cover image © Adobe Stock Photography.

Gravissimum Educationis (Declaration on Christian Education), no. 10, by Pope Paul VI (October 28, 1965) © Libreria Editrice Vaticana. Used with permission. All rights reserved.

Excerpts from *Code of Canon Law: New English Translation*, translation of *Codex Iuris Canonici*, 1998, © Canon Law Society of America, Washington, D.C. Used with permission. All rights reserved.

Sapientia Christiana (On Ecclesiastical Universities and Faculties), by Pope John Paul II (April 29, 1979) © Libreria Editrice Vaticana. Used with permission. All rights reserved.

Apostolic Constitution of the Supreme Pontiff John Paul II, *Ex corde Ecclesiae (On Catholic Colleges and Universities*, August 15, 1990), © 1990, Libreria Editrice Vaticana. Used with permission. All rights reserved.

First printing, March 2006

ISBN 978-1-57455-722-0

Contents

Introduction

Today Catholic universities in the United States often face the question, What is a Catholic university? Reflection on the rich guidance offered by the Church is useful to answer this question and to strengthen institutional identity in the process. The purpose of this compilation volume is to present key guiding documents provided by the Magisterium of the Church (the teaching office of the Holy Father) and the United States Conference of Catholic Bishops for the community of Catholic colleges and universities in the United States.

The Second Vatican Council's *Gravissimum Educationis* (*Declaration on Christian Education*, 1965) provides the vision for all Catholic education and specifically addresses Catholic higher education. This declaration is an important reminder of the continued responsibility that Catholic colleges and universities have in contributing to society through the influence and training of the Christian mind.

Specific guiding canons of the *Code of Canon Law* pertain to those working in Catholic higher education. By consulting these canons, one may gain a more complete understanding of other documents in this compilation; they provide the foundation upon which Pope John Paul II promulgated *Sapientia Christiana* and *Ex corde Ecclesiae*.

Pope John Paul II was instrumental in providing clarity of vision on the purpose and mission of the Catholic college/university. Promulgated early in his pontificate, *Sapientia Christiana* (*On Ecclesiastical Universities and Faculties*, 1979) was addressed specifically to ecclesiastical universities whose degrees are bestowed by pontifical authority. The pope maintained that certain basic norms must be followed by all such institutions to ensure that universal value is attached to pontifical degrees awarded by these institutions.

Pope John Paul II's apostolic constitution *Ex corde Ecclesiae* (*On Catholic Colleges and Universities*, 1990) is the most noteworthy recent document affecting the non-ecclesiastical Catholic university, published after lengthy discourse with the nine hundred Catholic institutions of higher learning throughout the world. It identified certain norms and expectations that Catholic colleges or universities must meet to be in accordance with the teachings of the Church on Catholic higher education. In this constitution, the Holy Father John Paul II declares the essential characteristics and elements of a Catholic college or university.

Ex corde Ecclesiae required that each country develop local and regional applications of the apostolic constitution, which were subject to approval by the local ecclesiastical authority. In 2000, seven bishops and eleven advisors in the United States created *The Application of "Ex corde Ecclesiae" for the United States* to develop the system for implementing *Ex corde Ecclesiae* in the United States. The *Application* was promulgated in May 2001.

Three additional documents in this volume provide specific guidance to the unique roles and responsibilities of the theologian in the Catholic academy: *Instruction on the Ecclesial Vocation of the Theologian*; *Guidelines Concerning the Academic Mandatum in Catholic Universities*; and *Doctrinal Responsibilities: Approaches to Promoting Cooperation and Resolving Misunderstandings Between Bishops and Theologians*. These documents are offered herein for all those involved in Catholic higher education, and in particular for bishops and theologians to use in their ongoing conversations as called for in *Ex corde Ecclesiae*.

Finally, the translations of the Profession of Faith and Oath of Fidelity are beneficial for readers to consider and reflect upon. These documents will be familiar for those in leadership positions in Catholic higher education and inspiring for those who may be unaware of the commitments made by those in such positions. These two texts embody the deep obligations and submission to the Magisterium of those who assume offices in the name of the Church.

The members of the Committee on Education of the United States Conference of Catholic Bishops echo the Holy Father in promoting Catholic mission and identity in Catholic colleges and universities. Therefore, the members of the committee take this opportunity to call attention to these significant documents and guidelines with the publication of this compilation, *Catholic Identity in Our Colleges and Universities*.

The official documents of the Church brought together in this volume provide rich teachings and offer the practical and theological foundations for the tradition of Catholic higher education. While all documents in this collection were previously published separately, they are now combined in one volume to allow for simple access and regular reference.

✝ Most Rev. Bishop Bernard J. Harrington, Bishop of Winona
Chairman, Committee on Education
United States Conference of Catholic Bishops

Gravissimum Educationis, no. 10

Declaration on Christian Education

PROCLAIMED BY
POPE PAUL VI
ON OCTOBER 28, 1965

10. Catholic Colleges and Universities

The Church is concerned also with schools of a higher level, especially colleges and universities. In those schools dependent on her she intends that by their very constitution individual subjects be pursued according to their own principles, method, and liberty of scientific inquiry, in such a way that an ever deeper understanding in these fields may be obtained and that, as questions that are new and current are raised and investigations carefully made according to the example of the doctors of the Church and especially of St. Thomas Aquinas,[31] there may be a deeper realization of the harmony of faith and science. Thus there is accomplished a public, enduring and pervasive influence of the Christian mind in the furtherance of culture and the students of these institutions are molded into men truly outstanding in their training, ready to undertake weighty responsibilities in society and witness to the faith in the world.[32]

In Catholic universities where there is no faculty of sacred theology there should be established an institute or chair of sacred theology in which there should be lectures suited to lay students. Since science advances by means of the investigations peculiar to higher scientific studies, special attention should be given in Catholic universities and colleges to institutes that serve primarily the development of scientific research.

Pope Paul VI, *Gravissimum Educationis (Declaration on Christian Education)*, October 28, 1965, no. 10. See http://www.vatican.va/archive/hist_councils/ii_vatican_council/documents/vat-ii_decl_19651028_gravissimum-educationis_en.html (accessed October 5, 2005).

The sacred synod heartily recommends that Catholic colleges and universities be conveniently located in different parts of the world, but in such a way that they are outstanding not for their numbers but for their pursuit of knowledge. Matriculation should be readily available to students of real promise, even though they be of slender means, especially to students from the newly emerging nations.

Since the destiny of society and of the Church itself is intimately linked with the progress of young people pursuing higher studies,[33] the pastors of the Church are to expend their energies not only on the spiritual life of students who attend Catholic universities, but, solicitous for the spiritual formation of all their children, they must see to it, after consultations between bishops, that even at universities that are not Catholic there should be associations and university centers under Catholic auspices in which priests, religious, and laity, carefully selected and prepared, should give abiding spiritual and intellectual assistance to the youth of the university. Whether in Catholic universities or others, young people of greater ability who seem suited for teaching or research should be specially helped and encouraged to undertake a teaching career.

NOTES

[31] Cf. Paul VI's allocution to the International Thomistic Congress, Sept. 10, 1965: *L'Osservatore Romano*, Sept. 13-14, 1965.

[32] Cf. Pius XII's allocution to teachers and students of French Institutes of Higher Catholic Education, Sept. 21, 1950: Discourses and Radio Messages, 12, pp. 219-221; letters to the 22nd congress of Pax Romana, Aug. 12, 1952: Discourses and Radio Messages, 14, pp. 567-569; John XXIII's allocution to the Federation of Catholic Universities, April 1, 1959: Discourses, Messages and Conversations, 1, Rome, 1960, pp. 226-229; Paul VI's allocution to the Academic Senate of the Catholic University of Milan, April 5, 1964: Encyclicals and Discourses of Paul VI, 2, Rome, 1964, pp. 438-443.

[33] Cf. Pius XII's allocution to the academic senate and students of the University of Rome, June 15, 1952: Discourses and Radio Messages, 14, p. 208: "The direction of today's society principally is placed in the mentality and hearts of the universities of today."

Canons Pertinent to Catholic Higher Education

From the *Code of Canon Law* (1998)

CHAPTER II.
CATHOLIC UNIVERSITIES AND OTHER INSTITUTES
OF HIGHER STUDIES

Can. 807 The Church has the right to erect and direct universities, which contribute to a more profound human culture, the fuller development of the human person, and the fulfillment of the teaching function of the Church.

Can. 808 Even if it is in fact Catholic, no university is to bear the title or name of *Catholic university* without the consent of competent ecclesiastical authority.

Can. 809 If it is possible and expedient, conferences of bishops are to take care that there are universities or at least faculties suitably spread through their territory, in which the various disciplines are studied and taught, with their academic autonomy preserved and in light of Catholic doctrine.

Can. 810 §1. The authority competent according to the statutes has the duty to make provision so that teachers are appointed in Catholic universities who besides their scientific and pedagogical qualifications are outstanding in integrity of doctrine and probity of life and that they are removed from their function when they lack these requirements; the manner of proceeding defined in the statutes is to be observed.

§2. The conferences of bishops and diocesan bishops concerned have the duty and right of being watchful so that the principles of Catholic doctrine are observed faithfully in these same universities.

Can. 811 §1. The competent ecclesiastical authority is to take care that in Catholic universities a faculty or institute or at least a chair of theology is erected in which classes are also given for lay students.

Code of Canon Law: New English Translation, translation of *Codex Iuris Canonici*, canons 807-821 and 833. Washington, DC: Canon Law Society of America, 1998.

§2. In individual Catholic universities, there are to be classes which especially treat those theological questions which are connected to the disciplines of their faculties.

Can. 812 Those who teach theological disciplines in any institutes of higher studies whatsoever must have a mandate from the competent ecclesiastical authority.

Can. 813 The diocesan bishop is to have earnest pastoral care for students, even by erecting a parish or at least by designating priests stably for this, and is to make provision that at universities, even non-Catholic ones, there are Catholic university centers which give assistance, especially spiritual assistance, to youth.

Can. 814 The prescripts established for universities apply equally to other institutes of higher learning.

CHAPTER III.
ECCLESIASTICAL UNIVERSITIES AND FACULTIES

Can. 815 Ecclesiastical universities or faculties, which are to investigate the sacred disciplines or those connected to the sacred and to instruct students scientifically in the same disciplines, are proper to the Church by virtue of its function to announce the revealed truth.

Can. 816 §1. Ecclesiastical universities and faculties can be established only through erection by the Apostolic See or with its approval; their higher direction also pertains to it.

§2. Individual ecclesiastical universities and faculties must have their own statutes and plan of studies approved by the Apostolic See.

Can. 817 No university or faculty which has not been erected or approved by the Apostolic See is able to confer academic degrees which have canonical effects in the Church.

Can. 818 The prescripts established for Catholic universities in cann. 810, 812, and 813 are also valid for ecclesiastical universities and faculties.

Can. 819 To the extent that the good of a diocese, a religious institute, or even the universal Church itself requires it, diocesan bishops or the competent superiors of the institutes must send to ecclesiastical universities or faculties youth, clerics, and members, who are outstanding in character, virtue, and talent.

Can. 820 The moderators and professors of ecclesiastical universities and faculties are to take care that the various faculties of the university offer mutual assistance as their subject matter allows and that there is mutual cooperation between their own university or faculty and other universities and faculties, even non-ecclesiastical ones, by which they work together for the greater advance of knowledge through common effort, meetings, coordinated scientific research, and other means.

Can. 821 The conference of bishops and the diocesan bishop are to make provision so that where possible, higher institutes of the religious sciences are established, namely, those which teach the theological disciplines and other disciplines which pertain to Christian culture.

TITLE V.
THE PROFESSION OF FAITH (Can. 833)

Can. 833 The following are obliged personally to make a profession of faith according to the formula approved by the Apostolic See:

6° in the presence of the local ordinary or his delegate and at the beginning of their function, pastors, the rector of a seminary, and teachers of theology and philosophy in seminaries; those to be promoted to the order of the diaconate;

7° in the presence of the grand chancellor or, in his absence, in the presence of the local ordinary or their delegates, the rector of an ecclesiastical or Catholic university, when the rector's function begins; in the presence of the rector if he is a priest or in the presence of the local ordinary or their delegates, teachers in any universities whatsoever who teach disciplines pertaining to faith or morals, when they begin their function.

Sapientia Christiana

On Ecclesiastical Universities and Faculties

APOSTOLIC CONSTITUTION

OF THE SUPREME PONTIFF

POPE JOHN PAUL II

(April 29, 1979)

FOREWORD

I

Christian wisdom, which the Church teaches by divine authority, continuously inspires the faithful of Christ zealously to endeavor to relate human affairs and activities with religious values in a single living synthesis. Under the direction of these values all things are mutually connected for the glory of God and the integral development of the human person, a development that includes both corporal and spiritual well-being.[1]

Indeed, the Church's mission of spreading the Gospel not only demands that the Good News be preached ever more widely and to ever greater numbers of men and women, but that the very power of the Gospel should permeate thought patterns, standards of judgment, and norms of behavior; in a word, it is necessary that the whole of human culture be steeped in the Gospel.[2]

The cultural atmosphere in which a human being lives has a great influence upon his or her way of thinking and, thus, of acting. Therefore, a division between faith and culture is more than a small impediment to evangelization, while a culture penetrated with the Christian spirit is an instrument that favors the spreading of the Good News.

Furthermore, the Gospel is intended for all peoples of every age and land and is not bound exclusively to any particular culture. It is valid for pervading

---

Pope John Paul II, *Sapientia Christiana* (*On Ecclesiastical Universities and Faculties*), April 29, 1979. See http://www.vatican.va/holy_father/john_paul_ii/apost_constitutions/documents/ hf_jp-ii_apc_15041979_sapientia-christiana_en.html (accessed October 20, 2005). Libreria Editrice Vaticana, 1979.

all cultures so as to illumine them with the light of divine revelation and to purify human conduct, renewing them in Christ.

For this reason, the Church of Christ strives to bring the Good News to every sector of humanity so as to be able to convert the consciences of human beings, both individually and collectively, and to fill with the light of the Gospel their works and undertakings, their entire lives, and, indeed, the whole of the social environment in which they are engaged. In this way the Church carries out her mission of evangelizing also by advancing human culture.[3]

II

In this activity of the Church with regard to culture, Catholic universities have had and still have special importance. By their nature they aim to secure that "the Christian outlook should acquire a public, stable and universal influence in the whole process of the promotion of higher culture."[4]

In fact, as my Predecessor Pope Pius XI recalled in the preface to the Apostolic Constitution *Deus Scientiarum Dominus*,[5] there arose within the Church, from her earliest period, didascaleia for imparting instruction in Christian wisdom so that people's lives and conduct might be formed. From these houses of Christian wisdom the most illustrious Fathers and Doctors of the Church, teachers, and ecclesiastical writers drew their knowledge.

With the passing of centuries schools were established in the neighborhood of cathedrals and monasteries, thanks especially to the zealous initiatives of bishops and monks. These schools imparted both ecclesiastical doctrine and secular culture, forming them into one whole. From these schools arose the universities, those glorious institutions of the Middle Ages which, from their beginning, had the Church as their most bountiful mother and patroness.

Subsequently, when civil authorities, to promote the common good, began and developed their own universities, the Church, loyal to her very nature, did not desist from founding and favoring such kinds of centers of learning and institutions of instruction. This is shown by the considerable number of Catholic universities established in recent times in nearly all parts of the world. Conscious of her worldwide salvific mission, the Church wishes to be especially joined to these centers of higher learning and she desires that they flourish everywhere and work effectively to make Christ's true message present in the field of human culture and to make it advance in that field.

In order that Catholic universities might better achieve this goal, my Predecessor Pope Pius XII sought to stimulate their united activity when, by his Apostolic Brief of July 27, 1949, he formally established the International Federation of Catholic Universities. It was "to include all Athenaea which the Holy See either has canonically erected or will in the future erect in the world, or will have explicitly recognized as following the norms of Catholic teaching and as completely in conformity with that teaching."[6]

The Second Vatican Council, for this reason, did not hesitate to affirm that "the Church devotes considerable care to schools of higher learning," and it strongly recommended that Catholic universities should "be established in suitable locations throughout the world" and that "the students of these institutions should be truly outstanding in learning, ready to shoulder duties of major responsibility in society and to witness to the faith before the world."[7] As the Church well knows, "the future of society and of the Church herself is closely bound up with the development of young people engaged in higher studies."[8]

III

It is not surprising, however, that among Catholic universities the Church has always promoted with special care Ecclesiastical Faculties and Universities, which is to say those concerned particularly with Christian revelation and questions connected therewith and which are therefore more closely connected with her mission of evangelization.

In the first place, the Church has entrusted to these Faculties the task of preparing with special care students for the priestly ministry, for teaching the sacred sciences, and for the more arduous tasks of the apostolate. It is also the task of these Faculties "to explore more profoundly the various areas of the sacred disciplines so that day by day a deeper understanding of sacred revelation will be developed, the heritage of Christian wisdom handed down by our ancestors will be more plainly brought into view, dialogue will be fostered with our separated brothers and sisters and with non-Christians, and solutions will be found for problems raised by doctrinal progress."[9]

In fact, new sciences and new discoveries pose new problems that involve the sacred disciplines and demand an answer. While carrying out their primary duty of attaining through theological research a deeper grasp of revealed truth, those engaged in the sacred sciences should therefore maintain contact with scholars of other disciplines, whether these are believers or not, and should try to evaluate and interpret the latters' affirmations and judge them in the light of revealed truth.[10]

From this assiduous contact with reality, theologians are also encouraged to seek a more suitable way of communicating doctrine to their contemporaries working in other various fields of knowledge, for "the deposit of faith, or the truths contained in our venerable doctrine, is one thing; quite another is the way in which these truths are formulated, while preserving the same sense and meaning."[11] This will be very useful so that among the People of God religious practice and uprightness of soul may proceed at an equal pace with the progress of science and technology, and so that, in pastoral work, the faithful may be gradually led to a purer and more mature life of faith.

The possibility of a connection with the mission of evangelization also exists in Faculties of other sciences which, although lacking a special link with Christian revelation, can still help considerably in the work of evangelizing. These are looked at by the Church precisely under this aspect when they are erected as Ecclesiastical Faculties. They therefore have a particular relationship with the Church's Hierarchy.

Thus, the Apostolic See, in carrying out its mission, is clearly aware of its right and duty to erect and promote Ecclesiastical Faculties dependent on itself, either with a separate existence or as parts of universities, Faculties destined for the education of both ecclesiastical and lay students. This See is very desirous that the whole People of God, under the guidance of their Shepherds, should cooperate to ensure that these centers of learning contribute effectively to the growth of the faith and of Christian life.

IV

Ecclesiastical Faculties—which are ordered to the common good of the Church and have a valuable relationship with the whole ecclesial community—ought to be conscious of their importance in the Church and of their participation in the ministry of the Church. Indeed, those Faculties which treat of matters that are close to Christian revelation should also be mindful of the orders which Christ, the Supreme Teacher, gave to His Church regarding this ministry: "Go therefore and make disciples of all nations, baptizing them in the name of the Father and of the Son and of the Holy Spirit, teaching them to observe all that I have commanded you" (Mt 28:19-20). From this it follows that there must be in these Faculties that adherence by which they are joined to the full doctrine of Christ, whose authentic guardian and interpreter has always been through the ages the Magisterium of the Church.

Bishops' Conferences in the individual nations and regions where these Faculties exist must diligently see to their care and progress, at the same time that they ceaselessly promote their fidelity to the Church's doctrine, so that these Faculties may bear witness before the whole community of the faithful to their wholehearted following of the above-mentioned command of Christ. This witness must always be borne both by the Faculty as such and by each and every member of the Faculty. Ecclesiastical Universities and Faculties have been constituted in the Church for the building up and perfecting of Christ's faithful, and they must always bear this in mind as a criterion in the carrying out of their work.

Teachers are invested with very weighty responsibility in fulfilling a special ministry of the word of God and in being instructors of the faith for the young. Let them, above all, therefore be for their students, and for the rest of the faithful, witnesses of the living truth of the Gospel and examples of fidelity to the Church. It is fitting to recall the serious words of Pope Paul VI: "The task of the theologian is carried out with a view to building up ecclesial communion so that the People of God may grow in the experience of faith."[12]

V

To attain these purposes, Ecclesiastical Faculties should be organized in such a way as to respond to the new demands of the present day. For this reason, the Second Vatican Council stated that their laws should be subjected to revision.[13]

In fact, the Apostolic Constitution *Deus Scientiarum Dominus*, promulgated by my Predecessor Pope Pius XI on May 24, 1931, did much in its time to renew higher ecclesiastical studies. However, as a result of changed circumstances, it now needs to be suitably adapted and altered.

In the course of nearly fifty years great changes have taken place not only in civil society but also in the Church herself. Important events, especially the Second Vatican Council, have occurred, events which have affected both the internal life of the Church and her external relationships with Christians of other churches, with non-Christians, and with non-believers, as well as with all those in favor of a more human civilization.

In addition, there is a steadily growing interest being shown in the theological sciences, not only among the clergy but also by lay people, who are attending theological schools in increasing numbers. These schools have, as a consequence, greatly multiplied in recent times.

Finally, a new attitude has arisen about the structure of universities and Faculties, both civil and ecclesiastical. This is a result of the justified desire for a university life open to greater participation, a desire felt by all those in any way involved in university life.

Nor can one ignore the great evolution that has taken place in pedagogical and didactic methods, which call for new ways of organizing studies. Then too there is the closer connection that is being felt more and more between various sciences and disciplines, as well as the desire for greater cooperation in the whole university environment.

To meet these new demands, the Sacred Congregation for Catholic Education, responding to the mandate received from the Council, already in 1967 began to study the question of renewal along the lines indicated by the Council. On May 20, 1968, it promulgated the *Normae quaedam ad Constitutionem Apostolicam "Deus Scientiarum Dominus" de studies academicis ecclesiasticis recognoscendam*, which has exercised a beneficial influence during recent years.

VI

Now, however, this work needs to be completed and perfected with a new law. This law, abrogating the Apostolic Constitution *Deus Scientiarum Dominus* and the Norms of Application attached to it, as well as the *Normae quaedam* published on May 20, 1968, by the Sacred Congregation for Catholic Education, includes some still valid elements from these documents, while laying down new norms whereby the renewal that has already successfully begun can be developed and completed.

Nobody is unaware of the difficulties that appear to impede the promulgation of a new Apostolic Constitution. In the first place, there is the "passage of time" which brings changes so rapidly that it seems impossible to lay down anything stable and permanent. Then there is the "diversity of places" which seems to call for a pluralism which would make it appear almost impossible to issue common norms, valid for all parts of the world.

Since however there exist Ecclesiastical Faculties throughout the world, which are erected and approved by the Holy See and which grant academic degrees in its name, it is necessary that a certain substantial unity be respected and that the requisites for gaining academic degrees be clearly laid down and have universal value. Things which are necessary and which are foreseen as being relatively stable must be set down by law, while at the same time a proper freedom must be left for introducing into the Statutes of the individual

Faculties further specifications, taking into account varying local conditions and the university customs obtaining in each region. In this way, legitimate progress in academic studies is neither hindered nor restricted, but rather is directed through right channels towards obtaining better results. Moreover, together with the legitimate differentiation of the Faculties, the unity of the Catholic Church in these centers of education will also be clear to everyone.

Therefore, the Sacred Congregation for Catholic Education, by command of my Predecessor Pope Paul VI, has consulted first of all, the Ecclesiastical Universities and Faculties themselves, then, the departments of the Roman Curia and the other bodies interested. After this, it established a commission of experts who, under the direction of the same Congregation, have carefully reviewed the legislation covering ecclesiastical academic studies.

This work has now been successfully completed, and Pope Paul VI was about to promulgate this Constitution, as he so ardently desired to do, when he died; likewise Pope John Paul I was prevented by sudden death from doing so. After long and careful consideration of the matter, I decree and lay down, by my apostolic authority, the following laws and norms.

Part One

GENERAL NORMS

Section I

Nature and Purpose of Ecclesiastical Universities and Faculties

Article 1. To carry out the ministry of evangelization given to the Church by Christ, the Church has the right and duty to erect and promote Universities and Faculties which depend upon herself.

Article 2. In this Constitution the terms Ecclesiastical Universities and Faculties mean those which have been canonically erected or approved by the Apostolic See, which foster and teach sacred doctrine and the sciences connected therewith, and which have the right to confer academic degrees by the authority of the Holy See.

Article 3. The purpose of Ecclesiastical Faculties are:

n. 1. through scientific research to cultivate and promote their own disciplines, and especially to deepen knowledge of Christian revelation and of matters connected with it, to enunciate systematically the truths contained therein, to consider in the light of revelation the most recent progress of the sciences, and to present them to the people of the present day in a manner adapted to various cultures;

n. 2. to train the students to a level of high qualification in their own disciplines, according to Catholic doctrine, to prepare them properly to face their tasks, and to promote the continuing permanent education of the ministers of the Church;

n. 3. to collaborate intensely, in accordance with their own nature and in close communion with the Hierarchy, with the local and the universal Church the whole work of evangelization.

Article 4. It is the duty of Bishops' Conferences to follow carefully the life and progress of Ecclesiastical Universities and Faculties, because of their special ecclesial importance.

Article 5. The canonical erection or approval of Ecclesiastical Universities and Faculties is reserved to the Sacred Congregation for Catholic Education, which governs them according to law.[14]

Article 6. Only Universities and Faculties canonically erected or approved by the Holy See and ordered according to the norms of this present Constitution have the right to confer academic degrees which have canonical value, with the exception of the special right of the Pontifical Biblical Commission.[15]

Article 7. The Statutes of each University or Faculty, which must be drawn up in accordance with the present Constitution, require approval by the Sacred Congregation for Catholic Education.

Article 8. Ecclesiastical Faculties erected or approved by the Holy See in non-ecclesiastical universities, which confer both canonical and civil academic degrees, must observe the prescriptions of the present Constitution, account being taken of the conventions signed by the Holy See with various nations or with the universities themselves.

Article 9. n. 1. Faculties which have not been canonically erected or approved by the Holy See may not confer academic degrees having canonical value.

n. 2. Academic degrees conferred by such Faculties, if they are to have value for some canonical effects only, require the recognition of the Sacred Congregation for Catholic Education.

n. 3. For this recognition to be given for individual degrees for a special reason, the conditions laid down by the Sacred Congregation must be fulfilled.

Article 10. For the correct carrying out of the present Constitution, the Norms of application issued by the Sacred Congregation for Catholic Education must be observed.

Section II

The Academic Community and Its Government

Article 11. n. 1. Since the University or Faculty forms a sort of community, all the people in it, either as individuals or as members of councils, must feel, each according to his or her own status, co-responsible for the common good and must strive to work for the institution's goals.

n. 2. Therefore, their rights and duties within the academic community must be accurately set down in the Statutes, to ensure that they are properly exercised within correctly established limits.

Article 12. The Chancellor represents the Holy See to the University or Faculty and equally the University or Faculty to the Holy See. He promotes the continuation and progress of the University or Faculty and he fosters its communion with the local and universal Church.

Article 13. n. 1. The Chancellor is the Prelate Ordinary on whom the University or Faculty legally depends, unless the Holy See established otherwise.

n. 2. Where conditions favor such a post, it is also possible to have a Vice-Chancellor, whose authority is determined in the Statutes.

Article 14. If the Chancellor is someone other than the local Ordinary, the statutory norms are to establish how the Ordinary and the Chancellor carry out their respective offices in mutual accord.

Article 15. The academic authorities are personal and collegial. Personal authorities are, in the first place, the Rector or President and the Dean. The collegial authorities are the various directive organisms or councils of the University or Faculty.

Article 16. The Statute of the University Faculty must very carefully set out the names and offices of the academic authorities, determining the way they are designated and their term of office, taking into account both the canonical nature of the individual University or Faculty and the university practice in the local area.

Article 17. Those designed as academic authorities are to be people who are truly knowledgeable about university life and, usually, who come from among the teachers of some Faculty.

Article 18. The Rector and the President are named, or at least confirmed, by the Sacred Congregation for Catholic Education.

Article 19. n. 1. The Statutes determine how the personal and the collegial authorities are to collaborate with each other, so that, carefully observing the principle of collegiality, especially in more serious matters and above all in those of an academic nature, the persons in authority will enjoy that exercise of power which really corresponds to their office.

n. 2. This applies, in the first place, to the Rector, who has the duty to govern the entire University and to promote, in a suitable way, its unity, cooperation, and progress.

Article 20. n. 1. When Faculties are parts of an Ecclesiastical University, their governance must be coordinated through the Statutes with the governance of the entire University in such a way that the good of the single Faculties is assured, at the same time that the good of the whole University is promoted and the cooperation of all the Faculties with each other is favored.

n. 2. The canonical exigencies of Ecclesiastical Faculties must be safeguarded even when such Faculties are inserted into non-Ecclesiastical universities.

Article 21. When a Faculty is joined to a seminary or college, the Statutes, while always having due concern for cooperation in everything pertaining to the students' good, must clearly and effectively provide that the academic direction and administration of the Faculty is correctly distinct from the governance and administration of the seminary or college.

Section III

Teachers

Article 22. In each Faculty there must be a number of teachers, especially permanent ones, which corresponds to the importance and development of the individual disciplines as well as to the proper care and profit of the students.

Article 23. There must be various ranks of teachers, determined in the Statutes, according to their measure of preparation, their insertion into the Faculty, their permanence, and their responsibility to the Faculty, taking into account the university practice of the local area.

Article 24. The Statutes are to define which authorities are responsible for hiring, naming, and promoting teachers, especially when it is a question of giving them a permanent position.

Article 25. n. 1. To be legitimately hired as a permanent teacher in a Faculty, a person must:

1) be distinguished by wealth of knowledge, witness of life, and a sense of responsibility;

2) have a suitable doctorate or equivalent title or exceptional and singular scientific accomplishment;

3) show documentary proof of suitability for doing scientific research, especially by a published dissertation;

4) demonstrate teaching ability.

n. 2. These requirements for taking on permanent teachers must be applied also, in proportionate measure, for hiring non-permanent ones.

n. 3. In hiring teachers, the scientific requirements in current force in the university practice of the local area should be taken into account.

Article 26. n. 1. All teachers of every rank must be marked by an upright life, integrity of doctrine, and devotion to duty, so that they can effectively contribute to the proper goals of an Ecclesiastical Faculty.

n. 2. Those who teach matters touching on faith and morals are to be conscious of their duty to carry out their work in full communion with the authentic Magisterium of the Church, above all, with that of the Roman Pontiff.[16]

Article 27 n. 1. Those who teach disciplines concerning faith or morals must receive, after making their profession of faith, a canonical mission from the Chancellor or his delegate, for they do not teach on their own authority but by virtue of the mission they have received from the Church. The other teachers must receive permission to teach from the Chancellor or his delegate.

n. 2. All teachers, before they are given a permanent post or before they are promoted to the highest category of teacher, or else in both cases, as the Statutes are to state, must receive a declaration of *nihil obstat* from the Holy See.

Article 28. Promotion to the higher ranks of teachers is to take place only after a suitable interval of time and with due reference to teaching skill, to research accomplished, to the publication of scientific works, to the spirit of cooperation in teaching and in research, and to commitment to the Faculty.

Article 29. The teachers, in order to carry out their tasks satisfactorily, must be free from other employment which cannot be reconciled with their duty to do research and to instruct, according to what the Statutes require for each rank of teacher.

Article 30. The Statutes must state:

a) when and under which conditions a teaching post ends;

b) for what reasons and in which ways a teacher can be suspended, or even deprived of his post, so as to safeguard suitably the rights of the teachers, of the Faculty or University, and, above all, of the students and also of the ecclesial community.

Section IV

Students

Article 31. Ecclesiastical Faculties are open to all, whether ecclesiastics or laity, who can legally give testimony to leading a moral life and to having completed the previous studies appropriate to enrolling in the Faculty.

Article 32. n. 1. To enroll in a Faculty in order to obtain an academic degree, one must present that kind of study title which would be necessary to permit enrollment in a civil university of one's own country or of the country where the Faculty is located.

n. 2. The Faculty, in its own Statutes, should determine what, besides what is contained in n. 1 above, is needed for entrance into its course of study, including ancient and modern language requirements.

Article 33. Students must faithfully observe the laws of the Faculty about the general program and about discipline—in the first place about the study program, class attendance, and examinations—as well as all that pertains to the life of the Faculty.

Article 34. The Statutes should define how the students, either individually or collectively, take part in the university community life in those aspects which can contribute to the common good of the Faculty or University.

Article 35. The Statutes should equally determine how the students can for serious reasons be suspended from certain rights or be deprived of them or even be expelled from the Faculty, in such a way that the rights of the student, of the Faculty or University, and also of the ecclesial community are appropriately protected.

Section V

Officials and Staff Assistants

Article 36. n. 1. In governing and administering a University or Faculty, the authorities are to be assisted by officials trained for various tasks.

n. 2. The officials are, first of all, the Secretary, the Librarian, and the Financial Procurator.

Article 37. There should also be other staff assistants who have the task of vigilance, order, and other duties, according to the needs of the University or Faculty.

Section VI

Study Program

Article 38. n. 1. In arranging the studies, the principles and norms which for different matters are contained in ecclesiastical documents, especially those of the Second Vatican Council, must be carefully observed. At the same time account must be taken of sound advances coming from scientific progress which can contribute to answering the questions being currently asked.

n. 2. In the single Faculties let that scientific method be used which corresponds to the needs of the individual sciences. Up-to-date didactic and teaching methods should be applied in an appropriate way, in order to bring about the personal involvement of the students and their suitable, active participation in their studies.

Article 39. n. 1. Following the norm of the Second Vatican Council, according to the nature of each Faculty:

1) just freedom[17] should be acknowledged in research and teaching so that true progress can be obtained in learning and understanding divine truth;

2) at the same time it is clear that:

   a) true freedom in teaching is necessarily contained within the limits of God's Word, as this is constantly taught by the Church's Magisterium,

   b) likewise, true freedom in research is necessarily based upon firm adherence to God's Word and deference to the Church's Magisterium, whose duty it is to interpret authentically the Word of God.

n. 2. Therefore, in such a weighty matter one must proceed with prudence, with trust, and without suspicion, at the same time with judgment and without rashness, especially in teaching, while working to harmonize studiously the necessities of science with the pastoral needs of the People of God.

Article 40. In each Faculty a curriculum of studies is to be suitably organized in steps or cycles, adapted to the material. They are usually as follows:

a) first, a general instruction is imparted, covering a coordinated presentation of all the disciplines, along with an introduction into scientific methodology;

b) next, one section of the disciplines is studied more profoundly, at the same time that the students practice scientific research more fully;

c) finally, there is progress toward scientific maturity, especially through a written work which truly makes a contribution to the advance of the science.

Article 41. n. 1. The disciplines which are absolutely necessary for the Faculty to achieve its purposes should be determined. Those also should be set out which in a different way are helpful to these purposes and, therefore, how these are suitably distinguished one from another.

n. 2. In each Faculty the disciplines should be arranged in such a way that they form an organic body, so as to serve the solid and coherent formation of the students and to facilitate collaboration by the teachers.

Article 42. Lectures, especially in the basic cycle, must be given, and the students must attend them, according to the norms to be determined in the Statutes.

Article 43. Practical exercises and seminars, mainly in the specialization cycle, must be assiduously carried on under the direction of the teachers. These ought to be constantly complemented by private study and frequent discussions with the teachers.

Article 44. The Statutes of the Faculty are to define which examinations or which equivalent tests the students are to take, whether written or oral, at the end of the semester, of the year, and especially of the cycle, so that their ability can be verified in regard to continuing in the Faculty and in regard to receiving academic degrees.

Article 45. Likewise the Statutes are to determine what value is to given for studies taken elsewhere, especially in regard to being dispensed from some disciplines or examinations or even in regard to reducing the curriculum, always, however, respecting the prescriptions of the Sacred Congregation for Catholic Education.

Section VII

Academic Degrees

Article 46. n. 1. After each cycle of the curriculum of studies, the suitable academic degree can be conferred, which must be established for each Faculty, with attention given to the duration of the cycle and to the disciplines taught in it.

n. 2. Therefore, according to the general and special norms of this Constitution, all degrees conferred and the conditions under which they are conferred are to be determined in the Statutes of the individual Faculties.

Article 47. n. 1. The academic degrees conferred by an Ecclesiastical Faculty are: Baccalaureate, Licentiate, and Doctorate.

n. 2. Special qualifications can be added to the names of these degrees according to the diversity of Faculties and the order of studies in the individual Faculties.

Article 48. Academic degrees can be given different names in the Statutes of the individual Faculties, taking account of the university practice in the local area, indicating, however, with clarity the equivalence these have with the names of the academic degrees above and maintaining uniformity among the Ecclesiastical Faculties of the same area.

Article 49. n. 1. Nobody can obtain an academic degree unless properly enrolled in a Faculty, completing the course of studies prescribed by the Statutes, and successfully passing the examinations or tests.

n. 2. Nobody can be admitted to the doctorate unless first having obtained the licentiate.

n. 3. A requisite for obtaining a doctorate, furthermore, is a doctoral dissertation that makes a real contribution to the progress of science, written under the direction of a teacher, publicly defended and collegially approved; the principal part, at least, must be published.

Article 50. n. 1. The doctorate is the academic degree which enables one to teach in a Faculty and which is therefore required for this purpose, the licentiate is the academic degree which enables one to teach in a major seminary or equivalent school and which is therefore required for this purpose.

n. 2. The academic degrees which are required for filling various ecclesiastical posts are to be stated by the competent ecclesiastical authority.

Article 51. An honorary doctorate can be conferred for special scientific merit or cultural accomplishment in promoting the ecclesiastical sciences.

Section VIII

Matters Related to Teaching

Article 52. In order to achieve its proper purposes, especially in regard to scientific research, each University or Faculty must have an adequate library, in keeping with the needs of the staff and students. It must be correctly organized and equipped with an appropriate catalogue.

Article 53. Through an annual allotment of money, the library must continually acquire books, old and new, as well as the principal reviews, so as to be able effectively to serve research, teaching of the disciplines, instructional needs, and the practical exercises and seminars.

Article 54. The library must be headed by a trained librarian, assisted by a suitable council. The librarian participates opportunely in the Council of the University or Faculty.

Article 55. n. 1. The Faculty must also have technical equipment, audio-visual materials, etc., to assist its didactic work.

n. 2. In relationship to the special nature and purpose of a University or Faculty, research institutions and scientific laboratories should also be available, as well as other apparatus needed for the accomplishment of its ends.

Section IX

Economic Matters

Article 56. A University or Faculty must have enough money to achieve its purposes properly. Its financial endowments and its property rights are to be carefully described.

Article 57. The Statutes are to determine the duty of the Financial Procurator as well as the part the Rector or President and the University or Faculty Council play in money matters, according to the norms of good economics and so as to preserve healthy administration.

Article 58. Teachers, officials, and staff assistants are to be paid a suitable remuneration, taking account of the customs of the local area, and also taking into consideration social security and insurance protection.

Article 59. Likewise, the Statutes are to determinate the general norms that will indicate the ways the students are to contribute to the expenses of the University or Faculty, by paying admission fees, yearly tuition, examination fees, and diploma fees.

Section X

Planning and Cooperation of Faculties

Article 60. n. 1. Great care must be given to the distribution, or as it is called, the planning of Universities and Faculties, so as to provide for their conservation, their progress, and their suitable distribution in different parts of the world.

n. 2. To accomplish this end, the Sacred Congregation for Catholic Education is to be helped by advice from the Bishops' Conferences and from a commission of experts.

Article 61. The erection or approval of a new University or Faculty is decided upon by the Sacred Congregation for Catholic Education when all the requirements are fulfilled. In this the Congregation listens to the local Ordinaries, the Bishops' Conference, and experts, especially from neighboring Faculties.

Article 62. n. 1. Affiliation of some institution with a Faculty for the purpose of being able to grant the bachelor's degree is approved by the Sacred Congregation for Catholic Education, after the conditions established by that same Sacred Congregation are fulfilled.

n. 2. It is highly desirable that theological study centers, whether diocesan or religious, be affiliated to a Faculty of Sacred Theology.

Article 63. Aggregation to a Faculty and incorporation into a Faculty by an institution for the purposes of also granting higher academic degrees is decided upon by the Sacred Congregation for Catholic Education, after the conditions established by that same Sacred Congregation are fulfilled.

Article 64. Cooperation between Faculties, whether of the same University or of the same region or of a wider territorial area, is to be diligently striven for. For this cooperation is of great help to the scientific research of the teachers and to the better formation of the students. It also fosters the advance of interdisciplinary collaboration, which appears ever more necessary in current times, as well as contributing to the development of complementarity among Faculties. It also helps to bring about the penetration by Christian wisdom of all culture.

Part Two
SPECIAL NORMS

Article 65. Besides the norms common to all Ecclesiastical Faculties, which are established in the first part of this Constitution, special norms are given here-under for certain of those Faculties, because of their particular nature and importance for the Church.

Section I
Faculty of Sacred Theology

Article 66. A Faculty of Sacred Theology has the aim of profoundly studying and systematically explaining, according to the scientific method proper to it, Catholic doctrine, derived with the greatest care from divine revelation. It has the further aim of carefully seeking the solution to human problems in the light of that same revelation.

Article 67. n. 1. The study of Sacred Scripture is, as it were, the soul of Sacred Theology, which rests upon the written Word of God together with living Tradition, as its perpetual foundation.[18]

n. 2. The individual theological disciplines are to be taught in such a way that, from their internal structure and from the proper object of each as well as from their connection with other disciplines, including philosophical ones and the sciences of man, the basic unity of theological instruction is quite clear, and in such a way that all the disciplines converge in a profound understanding of the mystery of Christ, so that this can be announced with greater effectiveness to the People of God and to all nations.

Article 68. n. 1. Revealed truth must be considered also in connection with contemporary, evolving, scientific accomplishments, so that it can be seen "how faith and reason give harmonious witness to the unity of all truth."[19] Also, its exposition is to be such that, without any change of the truth, there is adaptation to the nature and character of every culture, taking special account of the philosophy and the wisdom of various peoples. However, all syncretism and every kind of false particularism are to be excluded.[20]

n. 2. The positive values in the various cultures and philosophies are to be sought out, carefully examined, and taken up. However, systems and methods incompatible with Christian faith must not be accepted.

Article 69. Ecumenical questions are to be carefully treated, according to the norms of competent Church authorities.[21] Also to be carefully considered are relationships with non-Christian religions; and problems arising from contemporary atheism are to be scrupulously studied.

Article 70. In studying and teaching the Catholic doctrine, fidelity to the Magisterium of the Church is always to be emphasized. In the carrying out of teaching duties, especially in the basic cycle, those things are, above all, to be imparted which belong to the received patrimony of the Church. Hypothetical or personal opinions which come from new research are to be modestly presented as such.

Article 71. In presenting doctrine, those norms are to be followed which are in the documents of the Second Vatican Council,[22] as well as those found in more recent documents of the Holy See[23] insofar as these pertain to academic studies.

Article 72. The curriculum of studies of a Faculty of Sacred Theology comprises:

a) the first cycle, fundamentals, which lasts for five years or ten semesters, or else, when a previous two-year philosophy course is an entrance requirement, for three years. Besides a solid philosophical formation, which is a necessary propaedeutic for theological studies, the theological disciplines must be taught in such a way that what is presented is an organic exposition of the whole of Catholic doctrine, together with an introduction to theological scientific methodology.

The cycle ends with the academic degree of Baccalaureate or some other suitable degree as the Statutes of the Faculty determine.

b) the second cycle, specialization, which lasts for two years or four semesters. In this cycle the special disciplines are taught corresponding to the nature of the diverse specializations being undertaken. Also seminars and practical exercises are conducted for the acquisition of the ability to do scientific research.

The cycle concludes with the academic degree of specialized Licentiate.

c) the third cycle, in which for a suitable period of time scientific formation is brought to completion, especially through the writing of a doctrinal dissertation.

The cycle concludes with the academic degree of Doctorate.

Article 73. n. 1. To enroll in a Faculty of Sacred Theology, the student must have done the previous studies called for in accordance with article 32 of this Constitution.

n. 2. Where the first cycle of the Faculty lasts for only three years, the student must submit proof of having properly completed a two-year course in philosophy at a Faculty of Philosophy or at an approved institution.

Article 74. n. 1. A Faculty of Sacred Theology has the special duty of taking care of the scientific theological formation of those preparing for the priesthood or preparing to hold some ecclesiastical office.

n. 2. For this purpose, special courses suitable for seminarians should be offered. It is also appropriate for the Faculty itself to offer the "pastoral year" required for the priesthood, in addition to the five-year basic cycle. At the end of this year, a special Diploma may be conferred.

Section II

Faculty of Canon Law

Article 75. A Faculty of Canon Law, whether Latin or Oriental, has the aim of cultivating and promoting the juridical disciplines in the light of the law of the Gospel and of deeply instructing the students in these, so as to form researchers, teachers, and others who will be trained to hold special ecclesiastical posts.

Article 76. The curriculum of studies of a Faculty of Canon Law comprises:

a) the first cycle, lasting at least one year or two semesters, in which are studied the general fundamentals of Canon Law and those disciplines which are required for higher juridical formation;

b) the second cycle, lasting two years or four semesters, during which the entire *Code of Canon Law* is studied in depth, along with other disciplines having an affinity with it;

c) the third cycle, lasting at least a year or two semesters, in which juridical formation is completed and a doctoral dissertation is written.

Article 77. n. 1. With regard to the studies prescribed for the first cycle, the Faculty may make use of the studies done in another Faculty and which it can acknowledge as responding to its needs.

n. 2. The second cycle concludes with the Licentiate and the third with the Doctorate.

n. 3. The Statutes of the Faculty are to define the special requirements for the conferring of the academic degrees, observing the Norms of Application of the Sacred Congregation for Catholic Education.

Article 78. To enroll in a Faculty of Canon Law, the student must have done the previous studies called for in accordance with Article 32 of this Constitution.

Section III

Faculty of Philosophy

Article 79. n. 1. An Ecclesiastical Faculty of Philosophy has the aim of investigating philosophical problems according to scientific methodology, basing itself on a heritage of perennially valid philosophy.[24] It has to search for solutions in the light of natural reason and, furthermore, it has to demonstrate their consistency with the Christian view of the world, of man, and of God, placing in a proper light the relationship between philosophy and theology.

n. 2. Then, the students are to be instructed so as to make them ready to teach and to fill other suitable intellectual posts as well as to prepare them to promote Christian culture and to undertake a fruitful dialogue with the people of our time.

Article 80. In the teaching of philosophy, the relevant norms should be observed which are contained in the documents of the Second Vatican Council[25] and in other recent documents of the Holy See concerning academic studies.[26]

Article 81. The curriculum of studies of a Faculty of Philosophy comprises:

a) the first cycle, basics, in which for two years or four semesters an organic exposition of the various parts of philosophy is imparted, which includes treating the world, man, and God. It also includes the history of philosophy, together with an introduction into the method of scientific research;

b) the second cycle, the beginning of specialization, in which for two years or four semesters through special disciplines and seminars a more profound consideration is imparted in some sector of philosophy;

c) the third cycle, in which for a suitable period of time philosophical maturity is promoted, especially by means of writing a doctoral dissertation.

Article 82. The first cycle ends with the degree of Baccalaureate, the second with the specialized Licentiate, and the third with the Doctorate.

Article 83. To enroll in a Faculty of Philosophy, the student must have done the previous studies called for in accordance with Article 32 of the Constitution.

Section IV

Other Faculties

Article 84. Besides the Faculties of Sacred Theology, Canon Law, and Philosophy, other Faculties have been or can be canonically erected, according to the needs of the Church and with a view to attaining certain goals, as for instance:

a) a more profound study of certain sciences which are of greater importance to the theological, juridical, and philosophical disciplines;

b) the promotion of other sciences, first of all the humanities, which have a close connection with the theological disciplines or with the work of evangelization;

c) the cultivation of letters which provide a special help either to a better understanding of Christian revelation or else in carrying on the work of evangelizing;

d) finally, the more exacting preparation both of the clergy and laity for properly carrying out specialized apostolic tasks.

Article 85. In order to achieve the goals set down in the preceding article, the following Faculties or institutions "*ad instar Facultatis*" have already been erected and authorized to grant degrees by the Holy See itself:

- Christian archaeology
- Biblical studies and ancient Eastern studies
- Church history
- Christian and classical literature
- Liturgy
- Missiology
- Sacred Music
- Psychology
- Educational science or Pedagogy
- Religious science
- Social sciences
- Arabic studies and Islamology
- Mediaeval studies
- Oriental Ecclesiastical studies
- "*Utriusque Iuris*" (both canon and civil law)

Article 86. It belongs to the Sacred Congregation for Catholic Education to set out, in accordance with circumstances, special norms for these Faculties, just as has been done in the above sections for the Faculties of Sacred Theology, Canon Law, and Philosophy.

Article 87. The Faculties and Institutes for which special norms have not yet been set out must also draw up their own Statutes. These must conform to the General Norms established in the first part of this Constitution, and they must take into account the special nature and purpose proper to each of these Faculties or Institutes.

TRANSITIONAL NORMS

Article 88. This present Constitution comes into effect on the first day of the 1980-1981 academic year or of the 1981 academic year, according to the scholastic calendar in use in various places.

Article 89. Each University or Faculty must, before January 1, 1981, present its proper Statutes, revised according to this Constitution, to the Sacred Congregation for Catholic Education. If this is not done, its power to give academic degrees is, by this very fact, suspended.

Article 90. In each Faculty the studies must be arranged so that the students can acquire academic degrees according to the norms of this Constitution, immediately upon this Constitution coming into effect, preserving the students' previously acquired rights.

Article 91. The Statutes are to be approved experimentally for three years so that, when this period is completed, they may be perfected and approved definitively.

Article 92. Those Faculties which have a juridical connection with civil authorities may be given a longer period of time to revise their Statutes, providing that this is approved by the Sacred Congregation for Catholic Education.

Article 93. It is the task of the Sacred Congregation for Catholic Education, when, with the passage of time, circumstances shall require it, to propose changes to be introduced into this Constitution, so that this same Constitution may be continuously adapted to the needs of Ecclesiastical Faculties.

Article 94. All laws and customs presently obtaining which are in contradiction to this Constitution are abrogated, whether these are universal or local, even if they are worthy of special or individual mention. Likewise completely abrogated are all privileges hitherto granted by the Holy See to any person, whether physical or moral, if these are contrary to the prescriptions of this Constitution.

It is my will, finally, that this my Constitution be established, be valid, and be efficacious always and everywhere, fully and integrally in all its effects, that it be religiously observed by all to whom it pertains, anything to the contrary notwithstanding. If anyone, knowingly or unknowingly, acts otherwise than I have decreed, I order that this action is to be considered null and void.

Given at St. Peter's in Rome, the fifteenth day of April, the Solemnity of the Resurrection of our Lord Jesus Christ, in the year 1979, the first of my Pontificate.

NOTES
¹ Cf. Second Vatican Ecumenical Council, Pastoral Constitution on the Church in the Modern World *Gaudium et Spes*, 43ff.: AAS 58 (1966) pp. 1061ff.
² Cf. Apostolic Exhortation *Evangelii Nuntiandi*, 19-20: AAS 68 (1976) pp. 18ff.
³ Cf. ibid., 18: AAS 68 (1976) pp. 17f. and also Pastoral Constitution on the Church in the Modern World *Gaudium et Spes*, 58: AAS 58 (1966) p. 1079.
⁴ Cf. Second Vatican Ecumenical Council Declaration on Christian Education *Gravissimum Educationis*, 10: AAS 58 (1966) p. 737.
⁵ AAS 23 (1931) p. 241.
⁶ AAS 42 (1950) p. 387.
⁷ Declaration on Christian Education *Gravissimum Educationis*, 10: AAS 58 (1966) p. 737.
⁸ Ibid.
⁹ Ibid. 11: AAS 58 (1966) p. 738.
¹⁰ Pastoral Constitution on the Church in the Modern World *Gaudium et Spes*, 62: AAS 58 (1966) p. 1083.
¹¹ Cf. Pope John XXIII, Allocution at the opening of the Second Vatican Ecumenical Council: AAS 54 (1962) p. 792 and also the Pastoral Constitution on the Church in the Modern World *Gaudium et Spes*, 62: AAS 58 (1966) p. 1083.
¹² Pope Paul VI, Letter Le transfert a Louvain-la-Neuve to the Rector of the Catholic University of Louvain, September 13, 1975 (cf. L'Osservatore Romano, September 22-23, 1975). Also cf. Pope John Paul II, Encyclical Letter *Redemptor Hominis*, 19: AAS 71 (1979) pp. 305ff.
¹³ Declaration on Christian Education *Gravissimum Educationis*, 11: AAS 58 (1966) p. 738.
¹⁴ Cf. Apostolic Constitution *Regimini Ecclesiae Universae*, 78: AAS 59 (1967) p. 914.
¹⁵ Cf. Motu Proprio Sedula Cura: AAS 63 (1971) pp. 665ff. and also the Decree of the Pontifical Biblical Commission *Ratio periclitandae doctrinae*: AAS 67 (1975) pp. 153ff.
¹⁶ Cf. Second Vatican Ecumenical Council, Dogmatic Constitution on the Church *Lumen Gentium*, 25: AAS 57 (1965) pp. 29-31.
¹⁷ Second Vatican Ecumenical Council, Pastoral Constitution on the Church in the Modern World *Gaudium et Spes*, 59: AAS 58 (1966) p. 1080.
¹⁸ Second Vatican Ecumenical Council, Dogmatic Constitution on Divine Revelation *Dei Verbum* 24: AAS 58 (1966) p. 827.
¹⁹ Second Vatican Ecumenical Council, Declaration on Christian Education *Gravissimum Educationis*, 10: AAS 58 (1966) p. 737.
²⁰ Second Vatican Ecumenical Council, Decree on the Missionary Activity of the Church *Ad Gentes*, 22: AAS 58 (1966) pp. 973ff.
²¹ See the Ecumenical Directory, Second Part: AAS 62 (1970) pp. 705-724.
²² See especially Second Vatican Ecumenical Council, Dogmatic Constitution on Divine Revelation *Dei Verbum*: AAS 58 (1966) pp. 713ff.
²³ See especially the Letter of Pope Paul VI *Lumen Ecclesiae*, about St. Thomas Aquinas, of November 20, 1974: AAS 66 (1974) pp. 673ff. Also see the circular letters of the Sacred Congregation for Catholic Education: on the Theological Formation of Future Priests, February 22, 1976, on Canon Law Studies in Seminaries, March 1, 1975; and on Philosophical Studies, January 20, 1972.
²⁴ See Second Vatican Ecumenical Council, Decree on Priestly Formation *Optatam Totius*, 15: AAS 58 (1966) p. 722.
²⁵ Especially see the Second Vatican Council, Decree on Priestly Formation *Optatam Totius*: AAS 58 (1966) pp. 713ff. and the Declaration on Christian Education *Gravissimum Educationis*: AAS 58 (1966) pp. 728ff.
²⁶ See especially the letter of Pope Paul VI on St. Thomas Aquinas *Lumen Ecclesiae* of November 20, 1974: AAS 66 (1974) pp. 673ff. and the Circular letter of the Sacred Congregation for Catholic Education, On the Study of Philosophy in Seminaries, of January 20, 1972.

Norms of Application of the Sacred Congregation for Catholic Education for the Correct Implementation of the Apostolic Constitution Sapientia Christiana

The Sacred Congregation for Catholic Education, according to article 10 of the Apostolic Constitution *Sapientia Christiana*, presents to the Ecclesiastical Universities and Faculties the following Norms of Application and orders that they be faithfully observed.

Part One

GENERAL NORMS

Section I

Nature and Purpose of Ecclesiastical Universities and Faculties
(Apostolic Constitution, articles 1-10)

Article 1. By the term University or Faculty is understood also those Athenaea, Institutes, or Academic Centers which have been canonically erected or approved by the Holy See with the right to confer academic degrees by the authority of the same See.

Article 2. With a view to promoting scientific research, a strong recommendation is given for specialized research centers, scientific periodicals and collections, and meetings of learned societies.

Article 3. The tasks for which students can be prepared can be either strictly scientific, such as research or teaching, or else pastoral. Account must be taken of this diversity in the ordering of the studies and in the determining of the academic degrees, while always preserving the scientific nature of the studies for both.

Article 4. Active participation in the ministry of evangelization concerns the action of the Church in pastoral work, in ecumenism, and in missionary undertakings. It also extends to the understanding, defense, and diffusion of the faith. At the same time it extends to the whole context of culture and human society.

Article 5. Bishops' Conferences, joined to the Apostolic See in these matters also, are thus to follow carefully the Universities and Faculties:

1. together with the Chancellor they are to foster their progress and, while of course respecting the autonomy of science according to the mind of the Second Vatican Council, they are to be solicitous for their scientific and ecclesial condition;

2. with regard to common problems which occur within the boundaries of their own region, they are to help, inspire, and harmonize the activity of the Faculties;

3. bearing in mind the needs of the Church and the cultural progress of their own area, they are to take care that there exist an adequate number of such Faculties;

4. to do all this, they are to constitute among themselves a commission for this purpose, which should be helped by a committee of experts.

Article 6. In preparing the Statutes and Study Program, the norms in Appendix I of these directives must be kept in mind.

Article 7. n. 1. The canonical value of an academic degree means that such a degree enables one to assume an office in the Church for which a degree is required. This is, first of all, for teaching sacred sciences in Faculties, major seminaries, or equivalent schools.

n. 2. The condition to be fulfilled for the recognition of individual degrees mentioned in article 9 of the Apostolic Constitution, concern, first of all, besides the consent of the local or regional ecclesiastical authorities, the college of teachers, the study program, and the scientific helps used.

n. 3. Degrees thus recognized, for certain canonical effects only may never be considered simply as equal to canonical degrees.

Section II

The Academic Community and Its Government
(Apostolic Constitution, articles 11-21)

Article 8. The duty of the Chancellor is:

1. to promote continually the progress of the University or Faculty, to advance scientific progress, to ensure that Catholic doctrine is integrally followed, and to enforce the faithful implementation of the Statutes and the prescriptions of the Holy See;

2. to help ensure close relationships between all the different ranks and members of the community;

3. to propose to the Sacred Congregation for Catholic Education the names of those who are to be nominated or confirmed as Rector and President, as well as the names of the teachers for whom a nihil obstat is to be requested;

4. to receive the profession of faith of the Rector and President;

5. to give to or take away from the teachers the canonical mission or permission to teach, according to the norms of the Constitution;

6. to inform the Sacred Congregation for Catholic Education about more important matters and to send to that Congregation every three years a detailed report on the academic, moral, and economic condition of the University or Faculty.

Article 9. If the University or Faculty depends upon a collegial entity (for instance, on an Episcopal Conference), one designated member of the group is to exercise the office of Chancellor.

Article 10. The local Ordinary, if he is not the Chancellor, since he has the pastoral responsibility for his Diocese, is, whenever something in the University or Faculty is known to be contrary to doctrine, morals, or ecclesiastical discipline, to take the matter to the Chancellor so that the latter may take action. In case the Chancellor does nothing, the Ordinary may have recourse to the Holy See, without prejudice to his own obligation to provide personally for action in those cases which are more serious or urgent and which carry danger for his Diocese.

Article 11. What is contained in article 19 of the Constitution must be explained further in the proper Statutes of the individual Faculties, giving more weight, as the case may require, either to collegial or else to personal government, while always preserving both forms. Account should be taken of the university practice of the region where the Faculty is located or of the Religious Institute on which the Faculty may depend.

Article 12. Besides the University Council (Academic Senate) and the Faculty Council, both of which must everywhere exist even if under different names, the Statutes can suitably establish other special councils or commissions for scientific learning, teaching, discipline, finances, etc.

Article 13. n. 1. According to the Constitution, a Rector is one who presides over a University; a President is one who presides over an Institute or a Faculty which exists separately; a Dean is one who presides over a Faculty which is a part of a University.

n. 2. The Statutes are to fix a term of office for these persons (for instance, three years) and are to determine how and how many times their term can be renewed.

Article 14. The office of the Rector or President is:

1. to direct, promote, and coordinate all the activity of the academic community;

2. to be the representative of the University or of the Institute or Faculty existing separately;

3. to convoke the Council of the University or of the Institute or Faculty existing separately and preside over the same according to the norms of the Statutes;

4. to watch over the administration of temporalities;

5. to refer more important matters to the Chancellor;

6. to send, every year, a statistical summary to the Sacred Congregation for Catholic Education, according to the outline provided by that same Congregation.

Article 15. The Dean of the Faculty is:

1. to promote and coordinate all the activity of the Faculty, especially matters regarding studies, and to see to providing with due speed for their needs;

2. to convoke the Faculty Council and preside over it;

3. to admit or exclude students in the name of the Rector according to the norms of the Statutes;

4. to refer to the Rector what is done or proposed by the Faculty;

5. to see that the instructions of higher authorities are carried out.

Section III

Teachers
(Apostolic Constitution, articles 22-30)

Article 16. n. 1. Teachers who are permanently attached to a Faculty are, in the first place, those who are assumed in full and firm right and who are called Ordinary Professors; next come Extraordinary Professors. It can also be useful to have others according to university practice.

n. 2. Besides permanent teachers, there are other teachers who are designated by various titles, in the first place, those invited from other Faculties.

n. 3. Finally, it is also opportune to have Teaching Assistants to carry out certain academic functions.

Article 17. By a suitable doctorate is meant one that corresponds to the discipline that is being taught. If the discipline is sacred or connected with the sacred, the doctorate must be canonical. In the event that the doctorate is not canonical, the teacher will usually be required to have at least a canonical licentiate.

Article 18. Non-Catholic teachers, co-opted according to the norms of competent ecclesiastical authority,[1] require permission to teach from the Chancellor.

Article 19. n. 1. The Statutes must establish when a permanent status is conferred in relationship with the obtaining of the *nihil obstat* that must be procured in accordance with article 27 of the Constitution.

n. 2. The nihil obstat of the Holy See is the declaration that, in accordance with the Constitution and the special Statutes, there is nothing to impede a nomination which is proposed. If some impediment should exist, this will be communicated to the Chancellor who will listen to the teacher in regard to the matter.

n. 3. If particular circumstances of time or place impede the requesting of the nihil obstat from the Holy See, the Chancellor is to take counsel with the Sacred Congregation for Catholic Education to find a suitable solution.

n. 4. In Faculties which are under special concordat law the established norms are to be followed.

Article 20. The time interval between promotions, which must be at least three years, is to be set down in the Statutes.

Article 21. n. 1. Teachers, first of all the permanent ones, are to seek to collaborate with each other. It is also recommended that there be collaboration with the teachers of other Faculties, especially those with subjects that have an affinity or some connection with those of the Faculty.

n. 2. One cannot be at one and the same time a permanent teacher in more than one Faculty.

Article 22. n. 1. The Statutes are to set out with care the procedure in regard to the suspension or dismissal of a teacher, especially in matters concerning doctrine.

n. 2. Care must be taken that, first of all, these matters be settled between the Rector or President or Dean and the teacher himself. If they are not settled there, the matters should be dealt with by an appropriate Council or committee, so that the first examination of the facts be carried out within the University or Faculty itself. If this is not sufficient, the matters are to be referred to the Chancellor, who, with the help of experts, either of the University or the Faculty or from other places, must consider the matter and provide for a solution. The possibility remains open for recourse to the Holy See for a definitive solution, always allowing the teacher to explain and defend himself.

n. 3. However, in more grave or urgent cases for the good of the students and the faithful, the Chancellor can suspend the teacher for the duration of the regular procedure.

Article 23. Diocesan priests and Religious or those equivalent to Religious from whatever Institute, in order to be teachers in a Faculty or to remain as such, must have the consent of their proper Ordinary or Religious Superior, following the norms established in these matters by competent Church authority.

Section IV

Students
(Apostolic Constitution, articles 31-35)

Article 24. n. 1. Legal testimony, according to the norm of article 31 of the Constitution:

1) about a moral life is to be given, for clergy and seminarians, by their own Ordinary or his delegate; for all other persons by some ecclesiastic;

2) about previous studies in the study title required in accordance with article 32 of the Constitution.

n. 2. Since the studies required before entry into a University differ from one country to another, the Faculty has the right and duty to investigate whether all the disciplines have been studied which the Faculty itself considers necessary.

n. 3. A suitable knowledge of the Latin language is required for the Faculties of the sacred sciences, so that the students can understand and use the sources and the documents of the Church.[2]

n. 4. If one of the disciplines has been found not to have been studied or to have been studied in an insufficient way, the Faculty is to require that this be made up at a suitable time and verified by an examination.

Article 25. n. 1. Besides ordinary students, that is, those studying for academic degrees, extraordinary students can be admitted according to the norms determined in the Statutes.

n. 2. A person can be enrolled as an ordinary student in only one Faculty at a time.

Article 26. The transfer of a student from one Faculty to another can take place only at the beginning of the academic year or semester, after a careful examination of his academic and disciplinary situation. But in any event nobody can be given an academic degree unless all the requirements for the degree are fulfilled as the Statutes of the Faculty demand.

Article 27. In the norms which determine the suspension or the expulsion of a student from a Faculty, the student's right to defend himself must be safeguarded.

Section V

Officials and Staff Assistants
(Apostolic Constitution, articles 36-37)

Article 28. In the Statutes or in some other suitable document of the University or Faculty, the rights and duties of the Officials and Staff Assistants should be determined, as well as their participation in the community life of the University.

Section VI

Study Program
(Apostolic Constitution, articles 38-45)

Article 29. The Statutes of each Faculty must define which disciplines (principal and auxiliary) are obligatory and must be followed by all, and which are free or optional.

Article 30. Equally, the Statutes are to determine the practical exercises and seminars in which the students must not only be present but also actively work together with their colleagues and produce their own expositions.

Article 31. The lectures and practical exercises are to be suitably distributed so as to foster private study and personal work under the guidance of the teachers.

Article 32. n. 1. The Statutes are also to determine in what way the examiners are to make their judgments about candidates.

n. 2. In the final judgment about the candidates for the individual academic degrees, account is to be taken of all the marks received in the various tests in the same cycle, whether written or oral.

n. 3. In the examinations for the giving of degrees, especially the doctorate, it is also useful to invite examiners from outside the Faculty.

Article 33. The Statutes are to indicate the permanent curricula of studies which are to be instituted in a Faculty for special purposes and indicate the diplomas which are conferred at their conclusion.

Section VII

Academic Degrees
(Apostolic Constitution, articles 46-51)

Article 34. In Ecclesiastical Universities or Faculties which are canonically erected or approved, the academic degrees are given in the name of the Supreme Pontiff.

Article 35. The Statutes are to establish the necessary requisites for the preparation of the doctrinal dissertation and the norms for their public defense and publication.

Article 36. A copy of the published dissertation must be sent to the Sacred Congregation for Catholic Education. It is recommended that copies also be sent to other Ecclesiastical Faculties, at least those of the same region, which deal with the same science.

Article 37. Authentic documents regarding the conferring of degrees are to be signed by the Academic Authorities, according to the Statutes, and then are to be countersigned by the Secretary of the University or Faculty and have the appropriate seal affixed.

Article 38. Honorary doctorates are not to be conferred except with the consent of the Chancellor, who, having listened to the opinion of the University or Faculty Council, has obtained the *nihil obstat* of the Holy See.

Section VIII

Matters Relating to Teaching
(Apostolic Constitution, articles 52-55)

Article 39. The University or Faculty must have lecture halls which are truly functional and worthy and suited to the teaching of the disciplines and to the number of students.

Article 40. There must be a library open for consultation, in which the principle works for the scientific work of the teachers and students are available.

Article 41. Library norms are to be established in such a way that access and use is made easy for the students and teachers.

Article 42. Cooperation and coordination between libraries of the same city and region should be fostered.

Section IX

Economic Matters
(Apostolic Constitution, articles 56-59)

Article 43. To provide for continuous good administration, the authorities must inform themselves at set times about the financial situation and they must provide for careful, periodic audits.

Article 44. n. 1. Suitable ways should be found so that tuition fees do not keep from academic degrees gifted students who give good hope of one day being useful to the Church.

n. 2. Therefore care must be taken to set up forms of assistance for scholars, whatever their various names (scholarships, study burses, student subsidies, etc.), to be given to needy students.

Section X

Planning and Cooperation of Faculties
(Apostolic Constitution, articles 60-64)

Article 45. n. 1. In order to undertake the erection of a new University or Faculty, it is necessary that:

a) a true need or usefulness can be demonstrated, which cannot be satisfied either by affiliation, aggregation, or incorporation,

b) the necessary prerequisites are present, which are mainly:

  1) permanently engaged teachers who in number and quality respond to the nature and demands of a Faculty;

  2) a suitable number of students;

  3) a library with scientific apparatus and suitable buildings;

  4) economic means really sufficient for a University or Faculty;

c) the Statutes, together with the Study Program, be exhibited, which are in conformity to the Constitution and to these Norms of Application.

n. 2. The Sacred Congregation for Catholic Education—after listening to the advice first of the Bishops' Conference, mainly from the pastoral viewpoint, and next of experts, principally from nearby Faculties, mainly from the scientific viewpoint—will decide about the suitability of a new erection. This is commonly conceded at first experimentally for a period of time before being definitely confirmed.

Article 46. When, on the other hand, the approval of a University or Faculty is undertaken, this is to be done:

a) after the consent of both the Episcopal Conference and the local diocesan authority is obtained;

b) after the conditions stated in article 45, n. 1, under b) and c) are fulfilled.

Article 47. The conditions for affiliation regard, above all, the number and qualification of teachers, the study program, the library, and the duty of the affiliating Faculty to help the institution being affiliated. Therefore, this is usually granted only when the affiliating Faculty and the affiliated institution are in the same country or cultural region.

Article 48. n. 1. Aggregation is the linking with a Faculty of some Institute which embraces only the first and second cycle, for the purpose of granting the degrees corresponding to those cycles through the Faculty.

n. 2. Incorporation is the insertion into a Faculty of some Institute which embraces either the second or third cycle or both, for the purpose of granting the corresponding degrees through the Faculty.

n. 3. Aggregation and incorporation cannot be granted unless the Institute is specially equipped to grant degrees in such a way that there is a well-founded hope that, through the connection with the Faculty, the desired ends will be achieved.

Article 49. n. 1. Cooperation is to be fostered among the Ecclesiastical Faculties themselves by means of teacher exchanges, mutual communication of scientific work, and the promoting of common research for the benefit of the People of God.

n. 2. Cooperation with other Faculties, even those of non-Catholics, should be promoted, care always however being taken to preserve one's own identity.

Part Two

SPECIAL NORMS

Section I

Faculty of Sacred Theology
(Apostolic Constitution, articles 66-67)

Article 50. The theological disciplines are to be taught in such a way that their organic connection is made clear and that light be shed upon the various aspects or dimensions that pertain intrinsically to the nature of sacred doctrine. The chief ones are the biblical, patristic, historical, liturgical, and pastoral dimensions. The students are to be led to a deep grasp of the material, at the same time as they are led to form a personal synthesis, to acquire a mastery of the method of scientific research, and thus to become able to explain sacred doctrine appropriately.

Article 51. The obligatory disciplines are:

1. in the first cycle:

   a) the philosophical disciplines needed for theology, which are above all systematic philosophy together with its main parts and its historical evolution;

   b) the theological disciplines, namely:

   Sacred Scripture, introduction and exegesis

   fundamental theology, which also includes reference to ecumenism, non-Christian religions, and atheism

   dogmatic theology

   moral and spiritual theology

   pastoral theology

   liturgy

   Church history, patrology, archaeology

   Canon law

   c) the auxiliary disciplines, namely, some of the sciences of man and, besides Latin, the biblical languages insofar as they are required for the following cycles.

2. in the second cycle: the special disciplines established in various sections, according to the diverse specializations offered, along with the practical exercises and seminars, including written work.

3. in the third cycle: the Statutes are to determine if special disciplines are to be taught and which ones, together with practical exercises and seminars.

Article 52. In the fifth-year basic cycle, diligent care must be exercised that all the disciplines are taught with order, fullness, and with correct method, so that the student receives harmoniously and effectively a solid, organic, and complete basic instruction in theology, which will enable him either to go on to the next cycle's higher studies or to exercise some office in the Church.

Article 53. Besides examinations or equivalent tests for each discipline, at the end of the first and of the second cycle there is to be a comprehensive examination or equivalent test, so that the student proves that he has received the full and scientific formation demanded by the respective cycle.

Article 54. It belongs to the Faculty to determine under which conditions students who have completed a normal six-year philosophy/theology course in an ordinary seminary or in some other approved institution of higher learning may be admitted into the second cycle, taking account of their previous studies and, where necessary, prescribing special courses and examinations.

Section II

Faculty of Canon Law
(Apostolic Constitution, articles 76-79)

Article 55. In a Faculty of Canon Law, whether Latin or Oriental, there must be a careful setting forth both of the history and texts of ecclesiastical laws and of their disposition and connection.

Article 56. The obligatory disciplines are:

1. in the first cycle:

    a) the general fundamentals of canon law;

    b) the elements of Sacred Theology (especially of ecclesiology and sacramental theology) and of philosophy (especially ethics and natural law) which by their very nature are prerequisites for the study of canon law. It is useful to add elements from the sciences of man which are connected with the juridical sciences.

2. in the second cycle:

    a) the *Code of Canon Law* with all its various parts and the other canonical laws;

b) the connected disciplines, which are: the philosophy of law, the public law of the Church, fundamentals of Roman law, elements of civil law, the history of canon law. The student must also write a special dissertation.

3. in the third cycle: the Statutes are to determine which special disciplines and which practical exercises are to be prescribed, according to the nature of the Faculty and the needs of the students.

Article 57. n. 1. Whoever successfully completes the philosophy/theology curriculum in an ordinary seminary or in some other approved institution of higher learning, or who has already successfully completed the studies of the first cycle, may be admitted directly into the second cycle.

n. 2. A person who has already earned a doctorate in civil law, may be allowed, according to the judgment of the Faculty, to abbreviate the course, always maintaining however the obligation to pass all the examinations and tests required for receiving academic degrees.

Article 58. Besides examinations or equivalent tests for each discipline, at the end of the second cycle there is to be a comprehensive examination or equivalent test, whereby the student proves that he has received the full and scientific formation demanded by the cycle.

Section III

Faculty of Philosophy
(Apostolic Constitution, articles 79-83)

Article 59. n. 1. Philosophy is to be taught in such a way that the students in the basic cycle will come to a solid and coherent synthesis of doctrine, will learn to examine and judge the different systems of philosophy, and will also gradually become accustomed to personal philosophical reflection.

n. 2. All of the above is to be perfected in the second cycle, which begins specialization. In this cycle there is to be a deeper grasp of the determined object of philosophy and of the proper philosophical method.

Article 60. The obligatory disciplines are:

1. in the first cycle:

a) systematic philosophy (preceded by a general introduction) with its principal parts: philosophy of knowledge, natural philosophy, philosophy of man, philosophy of being (including natural theology) and moral philosophy;

b) history of philosophy, especially of modern philosophy, with a careful study of the systems which are exercising a major influence;

c) the auxiliary disciplines, namely selected natural and human sciences.

2. in the second cycle: the special disciplines established in various sections, according to the diverse specializations offered, along with practical exercises and seminars, including written work.

3. in the third cycle: the Statutes are to determine if special disciplines are to be taught and which ones, together with the practical exercises and seminars.

Article 61. Besides examinations or equivalent tests for each discipline, at the end of the first and second cycle there is to be a comprehensive examination or equivalent test whereby the student proves that he has received the full and scientific formation demanded by the respective cycle.

Article 62. It belongs to the Faculty to determine under what conditions students who have done a biennium of philosophy in an approved institution, or who have done a six-year philosophy/theology course in an ordinary seminary or equivalent school, may be admitted to the second cycle, taking account of their previous studies and, where necessary, prescribing special courses and examinations.

Section IV

Other Faculties
(Apostolic Constitution, articles 84-87)

Article 63. In accordance with article 86 of the Constitution, the Sacred Congregation for Catholic Education will gradually give special norms for the other Faculties, taking account of the experience already gained in these Faculties and Institutes.

Article 64. In the meantime, in Appendix II there is a list of the areas or divisions of ecclesiastical studies—besides the theological, canonical, and philosophical ones treated of in the three previous sections of these Norms of Application—which at the present time in the Church are ordered academically and are in existence as Faculties, Institutes ad instar, or Specialization Sections. The Sacred Congregation for Catholic Education will add to the list of these Sections when appropriate, indicating for these Sections their special purposes and the more important disciplines to be taught and researched.

His Holiness John Paul II, by divine Providence Pope, has ratified, confirmed, and ordered to be published each and every one of these Norms of Application, anything to the contrary notwithstanding.

Given from the offices of the Sacred Congregation for Catholic Education in Rome, April 29, the Memorial of St. Catherine of Siena, Virgin and Doctor of the Church, in the year of our Lord 1979.

Gabriel-Marie Cardinal GARRONE,
Prefect

Antonio Maria JAVIERRE ORTAS,
Titular Archbishop of Meta, Secretary

Appendix I
ACCORDING TO ARTICLE 6 OF THE NORMS OF APPLICATION
Norms for Drawing Up Statutes

Taking into account what is contained in the Apostolic Constitution and in the Norms of Application—and leaving to their own internal regulations what is of a particular or changeable nature—the Universities or Faculties must mainly deal with the following points in drawing up their Statutes:

1. The name, nature and purpose of the University or Faculty (with a brief history in the foreword).

2. The government—the Chancellor, the personal and collegial academic authorities: what their exact functions are; how the personal authorities are chosen and how long their term of office is; how the collegial authorities or the members of the Councils are chosen and how long their term is.

3. The teachers—what the minimum number of teachers is in each Faculty; into which ranks the permanent and non-permanent are divided; what requisites they must have; how they are hired, named, promoted, and how they cease functioning; their duties and rights.

4. The students—requisites for enrollment and their duties and rights.

5. The officials and staff assistants—their duties and rights.

6. The study program—what the order of studies is in each Faculty; how many cycles it has; what disciplines are taught; which are

obligatory, attendance at them; which seminars and practical exercises; which examinations and tests are to be given.

7. The academic degrees—which degrees are given in each Faculty and under what conditions.

8. Matters relating to teaching—the library; how its conservation and growth are provided for; other didactic helps and scientific laboratories, if required.

9. Economic matters—the financial endowment of the University or Faculty and its economic administration; norms for paying the staff assistants, teachers, and officials; student fees and payments, burses and scholarships.

10. Relationships with other Faculties and Institutes, etc.

Appendix II
ACCORDING TO ARTICLE 64 OF THE NORMS OF APPLICATION
Divisions of Ecclesiastical Studies as Now (1979) Existing in the Church

Note: These individual study Sectors are listed alphabetically (according to their Latin names) and in parenthesis is noted the academic organizational form (whether a Faculty or an Institute *ad instar* or a Sector of specialization) in which it now exists in some ecclesiastical academic center. Not listed are the studies of a theological, philosophical, or canonical kind which are treated in articles 51, 56, and 60 of the Norms of Application.

1. Arabic-Islamic studies (an Institute *ad instar*, a specialized Sector in a Theology Faculty).

2. Christian Archaeology studies (an Institute *ad instar*).

3. Studies in Atheism (a specialized Sector in a Theology and/or Philosophy Faculty).

4. Biblical studies (a Faculty of Biblical Science, a specialized Sector in a Theology Faculty).

5. Catechetical studies (a specialized Sector in a Theology or Education Faculty).

6. Ecclesiastical Oriental studies (a Faculty of Ecclesiastical Oriental Studies).

7. Education studies (a Faculty of Education).

8. Church History studies (a Faculty of Church History, a specialized Sector in a Theology Faculty).

9. Comparative Canonical-Civil Juridical studies (a Faculty of comparative civil law).

10. Classical and Christian Literary studies (a Faculty of Christian and Classical Letters).

11. Liturgical studies (a Faculty, a specialized Sector in a Theology Faculty).

12. Mariological studies (a specialized Sector in a Theology Faculty).

13. Medieval studies (an Institute *ad instar*, a specialized Sector in a Faculty of Theology or Canon Law or Philosophy).

14. Missiological studies (a Faculty of Missiology, a specialized Sector in a Theology Faculty).

15. Moral studies (a specialized Sector in a Theology Faculty).

16. Studies in Sacred Music (an Institute *ad instar*, a specialized Sector in a Theology Faculty).

17. Ecumenical studies (a specialized Sector in a Theology Faculty).

18. Ancient Oriental studies (a Faculty of Eastern Antiquity, a specialized Sector in a Theology or Philosophy Faculty).

19. Pedagogical studies (a Faculty of Pedagogy, a specialized Sector in a Philosophy or Education Faculty).

20. Pastoral studies (a specialized Sector in a Theology Faculty).

21. Patristic studies (a specialized Sector in a Theology Faculty).

22. Studies in Psychology (an Institute *ad instar*, a specialized Sector in a Faculty of Philosophy, or Pedagogy, or Education).

23. Studies in Religion and Religious Phenomenology (a specialized Sector in a Theology or Philosophy Faculty).

24. Catholic Religious studies (a Higher Institute of Religious Science).

25. Sociological studies (a Faculty of Social Science, a specialized Sector in a Faculty of Education).

26. Spirituality studies (a specialized Sector in a Theology Faculty).

27. Studies in the Theology of Religious Life (a specialized Sector in a Theology Faculty).

NOTES

[1] See the Ecumenical Directory, Second Part: AAS 62 (1970), pp. 705ff.

[2] The Second Vatican Ecumenical Council, Decree on Priestly Formation *Optatam Totius*, 13: AAS 58 (1966), p. 721 and the Chirograph of Pope Paul VI *Romani Sermonis*: AAS 68 (1976), pp. 481ff.

Ex corde Ecclesiae

On Catholic Universities

APOSTOLIC CONSTITUTION OF
THE SUPREME PONTIFF JOHN PAUL II

Introduction

1. BORN FROM THE HEART of the Church, a Catholic University is located in that course of tradition which may be traced back to the very origin of the University as an institution. It has always been recognized as an incomparable center of creativity and dissemination of knowledge for the good of humanity. By vocation, the *Universitas magistrorum et scholarium* is dedicated to research, to teaching and to the education of students who freely associate with their teachers in a common love of knowledge.[1] With every other University it shares that *gaudium de veritate*, so precious to Saint Augustine, which is that joy of searching for, discovering, and communicating truth[2] in every field of knowledge. A Catholic University's privileged task is "to unite existentially by intellectual effort two orders of reality that too frequently tend to be placed in opposition as though they were antithetical: the search for truth and the certainty of already knowing the fount of truth."[3]

2. For many years I myself was deeply enriched by the beneficial experience of university life: the ardent search for truth and its unselfish transmission to youth and to all those learning to think rigorously, so as to act rightly and to serve humanity better.

Therefore, I desire to share with everyone my profound respect for Catholic Universities, and to express my great appreciation for the work that is being done in them in the various spheres of knowledge. In a particular way, I wish to manifest my joy at the numerous meetings which the Lord has permitted me to have in the course of my apostolic journeys with the Catholic University communities of various continents. They are for me a

Apostolic Constitution of the Supreme Pontiff John Paul II, *Ex corde Ecclesiae* (*On Catholic Universities*, August 15, 1990). Libreria Editrice Vaticana, 1990.

lively and promising sign of the fecundity of the Christian mind in the heart of every culture. They give me a well-founded hope for a new flowering of Christian culture in the rich and varied context of our changing times, which certainly face serious challenges but which also bear so much promise under the action of the Spirit of truth and of love.

It is also my desire to express my pleasure and gratitude to the very many Catholic scholars engaged in teaching and research in non-Catholic Universities. Their task as academics and scientists, lived out in the light of the Christian faith, is to be considered precious for the good of the Universities in which they teach. Their presence, in fact, is a continuous stimulus to the selfless search for truth and for the wisdom that comes from above.

3. Since the beginning of this Pontificate, I have shared these ideas and sentiments with my closest collaborators, the Cardinals, with the Congregation for Catholic Education, and with men and women of culture throughout the world. In fact, the dialogue of the Church with the cultures of our times is that vital area where "the future of the Church and of the world is being played out as we conclude the twentieth century."[4] There is only one culture: that of man, by man, and for man.[5] And thanks to her Catholic Universities and their humanistic and scientific inheritance, the Church, expert in humanity, as my predecessor, Paul VI, expressed it at the United Nations,[6] explores the mysteries of humanity and of the world, clarifying them in the light of Revelation.

4. It is the honor and responsibility of a Catholic University to consecrate itself without reserve to *the cause of truth*. This is its way of serving at one and the same time both the dignity of man and the good of the Church, which has "an intimate conviction that truth is (its) real ally . . . and that knowledge and reason are sure ministers to faith."[7] Without in any way neglecting the acquisition of useful knowledge, a Catholic University is distinguished by its free search for the whole truth about nature, man, and God. The present age is in urgent need of this kind of disinterested service, namely of *proclaiming the meaning of truth*, that fundamental value without which freedom, justice and human dignity are extinguished. By means of a kind of universal humanism a Catholic University is completely dedicated to the research of all aspects of truth in their essential connection with the supreme Truth, who is God. It does this without fear but rather with enthusiasm, dedicating itself to every path of knowledge, aware of being preceded by him who is "the Way, the Truth, and the Life,"[8] the *Logos*, whose Spirit of intelligence and love enables the human person with his or her own intelligence to find the ultimate reality

of which he is the source and end and who alone is capable of giving fully that Wisdom without which the future of the world would be in danger.

5. It is in the context of the impartial search for truth that the relationship between faith and reason is brought to light and meaning. The invitation of Saint Augustine, *"Intellege ut credas; crede ut intellegas,"* [9] is relevant to Catholic Universities that are called to explore courageously the riches of Revelation and of nature so that the united endeavor of intelligence and faith will enable people to come to the full measure of their humanity, created in the image and likeness of God, renewed even more marvelously, after sin, in Christ, and called to shine forth in the light of the Spirit.

6. Through the encounter which it establishes between the unfathomable richness of the salvific message of the Gospel and the variety and immensity of the fields of knowledge in which that richness is incarnated by it, a Catholic University enables the Church to institute an incomparably fertile dialogue with people of every culture. Man's life is given dignity by culture, and, while he finds his fullness in Christ, there can be no doubt that the Gospel which reaches and renews him in every dimension is also fruitful for the culture in which he lives. •

7. In the world today, characterized by such rapid developments in science and technology, the tasks of a Catholic University assume an ever greater importance and urgency. Scientific and technological discoveries create an enormous economic and industrial growth, but they also inescapably require the correspondingly necessary *search for meaning* in order to guarantee that the new discoveries be used for the authentic good of individuals and of human society as a whole. If it is the responsibility of every University to search for such meaning, a Catholic University is called in a particular way to respond to this need: its Christian inspiration enables it to include the moral, spiritual, and religious dimension in its research, and to evaluate the attainments of science and technology in the perspective of the totality of the human person.

In this context, Catholic Universities are called to a continuous renewal, both as "Universities" and as "Catholic." For, "What is at stake is the *very meaning of scientific and technological research, of social life and of culture,* but, on an even more profound level, what is at stake is *the very meaning of the human person.*"[10] Such renewal requires a clear awareness that, by its Catholic character, a University is made more capable of conducting an *impartial* search for truth, a search that is neither subordinated to nor conditioned by particular interests of any kind.

8. Having already dedicated the Apostolic Constitution *Sapientia Christiana* to Ecclesiastical Faculties and Universities,[11] I then felt obliged to

propose an analogous Document for Catholic Universities as a sort of "magna carta," enriched by the long and fruitful experience of the Church in the realm of Universities and open to the promise of future achievements that will require courageous creativity and rigorous fidelity.

9. The present Document is addressed especially to those who conduct Catholic Universities, to the respective academic communities, to all those who have an interest in them, particularly the Bishops, Religious Congregations, and ecclesial *Institutions*, and to the numerous laity who are committed to the great mission of higher education. Its purpose is that "the Christian mind may achieve, as it were, a public, persistent, and universal presence in the whole enterprise of advancing higher culture and that the students of these institutions become people outstanding in learning, ready to shoulder society's heavier burdens and to witness the faith to the world."[12]

10. In addition to Catholic Universities, I also turn to the many Catholic Institutions of higher education. According to their nature and proper objectives, they share some or all of the characteristics of a University and they offer their own contribution to the Church and to society, whether through research, education or professional training. While this Document specifically concerns Catholic Universities, it is also meant to include all Catholic Institutions of higher education engaged in instilling the Gospel message of Christ in souls and cultures.

Therefore, it is with great trust and hope that I invite all Catholic Universities to pursue their irreplaceable task. Their mission appears increasingly necessary for the encounter of the Church with the development of the sciences and with the cultures of our age.

Together with all my brother Bishops who share pastoral responsibility with me, I would like to manifest my deep conviction that a Catholic University is without any doubt one of the best instruments that the Church offers to our age which is searching for certainty and wisdom. Having the mission of bringing the Good News to everyone, the Church should never fail to interest herself in this Institution. By research and teaching, Catholic Universities assist the Church in the manner most appropriate to modern times to find cultural treasures both old and new, "*nova et vetera*," according to the words of Jesus.[13]

11. Finally, I turn to the whole Church, convinced that Catholic Universities are essential to her growth and to the development of Christian culture and human progress. For this reason, the entire ecclesial Community is invited to give its support to Catholic Institutions of higher education and to assist them in their process of development and renewal. It is invited in a

special way to guard the rights and freedom of these Institutions in civil society, and to offer them economic aid, especially in those countries where they have more urgent need of it, and to furnish assistance in founding new Catholic Universities wherever this might be necessary.

My hope is that these prescriptions, based on the teaching of Vatican Council II and the directives of the *Code of Canon Law*, will enable Catholic Universities and other Institutes of higher studies to fulfill their indispensable mission in the new advent of grace that is opening up to the new Millennium.

Part I
IDENTITY AND MISSION
A. The Identity of a Catholic University

1. Nature and Objectives

12. Every Catholic University, *as a university*, is an academic community which, in a rigorous and critical fashion, assists in the protection and advancement of human dignity and of a cultural heritage through research, teaching, and various services offered to the local, national, and international communities.[14] It possesses that institutional autonomy necessary to perform its functions effectively and guarantees its members academic freedom, so long as the rights of the individual person and of the community are preserved within the confines of the truth and the common good.[15]

13. Since the objective of a Catholic University is to assure in an institutional manner a Christian presence in the university world confronting the great problems of society and culture,[16] every Catholic University, as *Catholic*, must have the following *essential characteristics:*

"1. a Christian inspiration not only of individuals but of the university community as such;

2. a continuing reflection in the light of the Catholic faith upon the growing treasury of human knowledge, to which it seeks to contribute by its own research;

3. fidelity to the Christian message as it comes to us through the Church;

4. an *institutional commitment* to the service of the people of God and of the human family in their pilgrimage to the transcendent goal which gives meaning to life."[17]

14. "In the light of these four characteristics, it is evident that besides the teaching, research, and services common to all Universities, a Catholic University, by *institutional commitment*, brings to its task the inspiration and light of the *Christian message*. In a Catholic University, therefore, Catholic ideals, attitudes, and principles penetrate and inform university activities in accordance with the proper nature and autonomy of these activities. In a word, being both a University and Catholic, it must be both a community of scholars representing various branches of human knowledge, and an academic institution in which Catholicism is vitally present and operative."[18]

15. A Catholic University, therefore, is a place of research, where scholars *scrutinize reality* with the methods proper to each academic discipline, and so contribute to the treasury of human knowledge. Each individual discipline is studied in a systematic manner; moreover, the various disciplines are brought into dialogue for their mutual enhancement.

In addition to assisting men and women in their continuing quest for the truth, this research provides an effective witness, especially necessary today, to the Church's belief in the intrinsic value of knowledge and research.

In a Catholic University, research necessarily includes (a) the search for an *integration of knowledge*, (b) a *dialogue between faith and reason*, (c) an *ethical concern*, and (d) a *theological perspective*.

16. *Integration of knowledge* is a process, one which will always remain incomplete; moreover, the explosion of knowledge in recent decades, together with the rigid compartmentalization of knowledge within individual academic disciplines, makes the task increasingly difficult. But a University, and especially a Catholic University, "has to be a 'living union' of individual organisms dedicated to the search for truth. . . . It is necessary to work towards a higher synthesis of knowledge, in which alone lies the possibility of satisfying that thirst for truth which is profoundly inscribed on the heart of the human person."[19] Aided by the specific contributions of philosophy and theology, university scholars will be engaged in a constant effort to determine the relative place and meaning of each of the various disciplines within the context of a vision of the human person and the world that is enlightened by the Gospel, and therefore by a faith in Christ, the *Logos*, as the center of creation and of human history.

17. In promoting this integration of knowledge, a specific part of a Catholic University's task is to promote *dialogue between faith and reason*, so that it can be seen more profoundly how faith and reason bear harmonious witness to the unity of all truth. While each academic discipline retains its own integrity and has its own methods, this dialogue demonstrates that

"methodical research within every branch of learning, when carried out in a truly scientific manner and in accord with moral norms, can never truly conflict with faith. For the things of the earth and the concerns of faith derive from the same God."[20] A vital interaction of two distinct levels of coming to know the one truth leads to a greater love for truth itself, and contributes to a more comprehensive understanding of the meaning of human life and of the purpose of God's creation.

18. Because knowledge is meant to serve the human person, research in a Catholic University is always carried out with a concern for the *ethical* and *moral implications* both of its methods and of its discoveries. This concern, while it must be present in all research, is particularly important in the areas of science and technology. "It is essential that we be convinced of the priority of the ethical over the technical, of the primacy of the person over things, of the superiority of the spirit over matter. The cause of the human person will only be served if knowledge is joined to conscience. Men and women of science will truly aid humanity only if they preserve 'the sense of the transcendence of the human person over the world and of God over the human person.'"[21]

19. *Theology* plays a particularly important role in the search for a synthesis of knowledge as well as in the dialogue between faith and reason. It serves all other disciplines in their search for meaning, not only by helping them to investigate how their discoveries will affect individuals and society but also by bringing a perspective and an orientation not contained within their own methodologies. In turn, interaction with these other disciplines and their discoveries enriches theology, offering it a better understanding of the world today, and making theological research more relevant to current needs. Because of its specific importance among the academic disciplines, every Catholic University should have a faculty, or at least a chair, of theology.[22]

20. Given the close connection between research and teaching, the research qualities indicated above will have their influence on all teaching. While each discipline is taught systematically and according to its own methods, *interdisciplinary studies,* assisted by a careful and thorough study of philosophy and theology, enable students to acquire an organic vision of reality and to develop a continuing desire for intellectual progress. In the communication of knowledge, emphasis is then placed on how *human reason in its reflection* opens to increasingly broader questions, and how the complete answer to them can only come from above through faith. Furthermore, the *moral implications* that are present in each discipline are examined as an integral part of the teaching of that discipline so that the entire educative process be directed towards the whole development of the person. Finally, Catholic theology,

taught in a manner faithful to Scripture, Tradition, and the Church's Magisterium, provides an awareness of the Gospel principles which will enrich the meaning of human life and give it a new dignity.

Through research and teaching the students are educated in the various disciplines so as to become truly competent in the specific sectors in which they will devote themselves to the service of society and of the Church, but at the same time prepared to give the witness of their faith to the world.

2. The University Community

21. A Catholic University pursues its objectives through its formation of an authentic human community animated by the spirit of Christ. The source of its unity springs from a common dedication to the truth, a common vision of the dignity of the human person and, ultimately, the person and message of Christ which gives the Institution its distinctive character. As a result of this inspiration, the community is animated by a spirit of freedom and charity; it is characterized by mutual respect, sincere dialogue, and protection of the rights of individuals. It assists each of its members to achieve wholeness as human persons; in turn, everyone in the community helps in promoting unity, and each one, according to his or her role and capacity, contributes towards decisions which affect the community, and also towards maintaining and strengthening the distinctive Catholic character of the Institution.

22. *University teachers* should seek to improve their competence and endeavor to set the content, objectives, methods, and results of research in an individual discipline within the framework of a coherent world vision. Christians among the teachers are called to be witnesses and educators of authentic Christian life, which evidences attained integration between faith and life, and between professional competence and Christian wisdom. All teachers are to be inspired by academic ideals and by the principles of an authentically human life.

23. *Students* are challenged to pursue an education that combines excellence in humanistic and cultural development with specialized professional training. Most especially, they are challenged to continue the search for truth and for meaning throughout their lives, since "the human spirit must be cultivated in such a way that there results a growth in its ability to wonder, to understand, to contemplate, to make personal judgments, and to develop a religious, moral, and social sense."[23] This enables them to acquire or, if they have already done so, to deepen a Christian way of life that is authentic. They should realize the responsibility of their professional life, the enthusiasm of

being the trained 'leaders' of tomorrow, of being witnesses to Christ in whatever place they may exercise their profession.

24. *Directors* and *administrators* in a Catholic University promote the constant growth of the University and its community through a leadership of service; the dedication and witness of the *non-academic staff* are vital for the identity and life of the University.

25. Many Catholic Universities were founded by Religious Congregations, and continue to depend on their support; those Religious Congregations dedicated to the apostolate of higher education are urged to assist these Institutions in the renewal of their commitment, and to continue to prepare religious men and women who can positively contribute to the mission of a Catholic University.

Lay people have found in university activities a means by which they too could exercise an important apostolic role in the Church and, in most Catholic Universities today, the academic community is largely composed of laity; in increasing numbers, lay men and women are assuming important functions and responsibilities for the direction of these Institutions. These lay Catholics are responding to the Church's call "to be present, as signs of courage and intellectual creativity, in the privileged places of culture, that is, the world of education—school and university."[24] The future of Catholic Universities depends to a great extent on the competent and dedicated service of lay Catholics. The Church sees their developing presence in these institutions both as a sign of hope and as a confirmation of the irreplaceable lay vocation in the Church and in the world, confident that lay people will, in the exercise of their own distinctive role, "illumine and organize these (temporal) affairs in such a way that they always start out, develop, and continue according to Christ's mind, to the praise of the Creator and the Redeemer."[25]

26. The university community of many Catholic institutions includes members of other Churches, ecclesial communities and religions, and also those who profess no religious belief. These men and women offer their training and experience in furthering the various academic disciplines or other university tasks.

3. The Catholic University in the Church

27. Every Catholic University, without ceasing to be a University, has a relationship to the Church that is essential to its institutional identity. As such, it participates most directly in the life of the local Church in which it is situated; at the same time, because it is an academic institution and therefore a part of the international community of scholarship and inquiry, each insti-

tution participates in and contributes to the life and the mission of the universal Church, assuming consequently a special bond with the Holy See by reason of the service to unity which it is called to render to the whole Church. One consequence of its essential relationship to the Church is that the *institutional* fidelity of the University to the Christian message includes a recognition of and adherence to the teaching authority of the Church in matters of faith and morals. Catholic members of the university community are also called to a personal fidelity to the Church with all that this implies. Non-Catholic members are required to respect the Catholic character of the University, while the University in turn respects their religious liberty.[26]

28. Bishops have a particular responsibility to promote Catholic Universities, and especially to promote and assist in the preservation and strengthening of their Catholic identity, including the protection of their Catholic identity in relation to civil authorities. This will be achieved more effectively if close personal and pastoral relationships exist between University and Church authorities, characterized by mutual trust, close and consistent cooperation, and continuing dialogue. Even when they do not enter directly into the internal governance of the University, Bishops "should be seen not as external agents but as participants in the life of the Catholic University."[27]

29. The Church, accepting "the legitimate autonomy of human culture and especially of the sciences," recognizes the academic freedom of scholars in each discipline in accordance with its own principles and proper methods,[28] and within the confines of the truth and the common good.

Theology has its legitimate place in the University alongside other disciplines. It has proper principles and methods which define it as a branch of knowledge. Theologians enjoy this same freedom so long as they are faithful to these principles and methods.

Bishops should encourage the creative work of theologians. They serve the Church through research done in a way that respects theological method. They seek to understand better, further develop, and more effectively communicate the meaning of Christian Revelation as transmitted in Scripture and Tradition and in the Church's Magisterium. They also investigate the ways in which theology can shed light on specific questions raised by contemporary culture. At the same time, since theology seeks an understanding of revealed truth whose authentic interpretation is entrusted to the Bishops of the Church,[29] it is intrinsic to the principles and methods of their research and teaching in their academic discipline that theologians respect the authority of the Bishops, and assent to Catholic doctrine according to the degree of authority with which it is taught.[30] Because of their interrelated roles, dialogue between Bishops and theologians is essential; this is especially true today, when the results of research are so quickly and so widely communicated through the media.[31]

B. The Mission of Service of a Catholic University

30. The basic mission of a University is a continuous quest for truth through its research, and the preservation and communication of knowledge for the good of society. A Catholic University participates in this mission with its own specific characteristics and purposes.

1. Service to Church and Society

31. Through teaching and research, a Catholic University offers an indispensable contribution to the Church. In fact, it prepares men and women who, inspired by Christian principles and helped to live their Christian vocation in a mature and responsible manner, will be able to assume positions of responsibility in the Church. Moreover, by offering the results of its scientific research, a Catholic University will be able to help the Church respond to the problems and needs of this age.

32. A Catholic University, as any University, is immersed in human society; as an extension of its service to the Church, and always within its proper competence, it is called on to become an ever more effective instrument of cultural progress for individuals as well as for society. Included among its research activities, therefore, will be a study of *serious contemporary problems* in areas such as the dignity of human life, the promotion of justice for all, the quality of personal and family life, the protection of nature, the search for peace and political stability, a more just sharing in the world's resources, and a new economic and political order that will better serve the human community at a national and international level. University research will seek to discover the roots and causes of the serious problems of our time, paying special attention to their ethical and religious dimensions.

If need be, a Catholic University must have the courage to speak uncomfortable truths which do not please public opinion, but which are necessary to safeguard the authentic good of society.

33. A specific priority is the need to examine and evaluate the predominant values and norms of modern society and culture in a Christian perspective, and the responsibility to try to communicate to society those *ethical and religious*

principles which give full meaning to human life. In this way a University can contribute further to the development of a true Christian anthropology, founded on the person of Christ, which will bring the dynamism of the creation and redemption to bear on reality and on the correct solution to the problems of life.

34. The Christian spirit of service to others for the *promotion of social justice* is of particular importance for each Catholic University, to be shared by its teachers and developed in its students. The Church is firmly committed to the integral growth of all men and women.[32] The Gospel, interpreted in the social teachings of the Church, is an urgent call to promote "the development of those peoples who are striving to escape from hunger, misery, endemic diseases, and ignorance; of those who are looking for a wider share in the benefits of civilization and a more active improvement of their human qualities; of those who are aiming purposefully at their complete fulfillment."[33] Every Catholic University feels responsible to contribute concretely to the progress of the society within which it works: for example, it will be capable of searching for ways to make university education accessible to all those who are able to benefit from it, especially the poor or members of minority groups who customarily have been deprived of it. A Catholic University also has the responsibility, to the degree that it is able, to help to promote the development of the emerging nations.

35. In its attempts to resolve these complex issues that touch on so many different dimensions of human life and of society, a Catholic University will insist on cooperation among the different academic disciplines, each offering its distinct contribution in the search for solutions; moreover, since the economic and personal resources of a single Institution are limited, cooperation in *common research projects* among Catholic Universities, as well as with other private and governmental institutions, is imperative. In this regard, and also in what pertains to the other fields of the specific activity of a Catholic University, the role played by various national and international associations of Catholic Universities is to be emphasized. Among these associations the mission of *The International Federation of Catholic Universities,* founded by the Holy See,[34] is particularly to be remembered. The Holy See anticipates further fruitful collaboration with this Federation.

36. Through programs of *continuing education* offered to the wider community, by making its scholars available for consulting services, by taking advantage of modern means of communication, and in a variety of other ways, a Catholic University can assist in making the growing body of human knowledge and a developing understanding of the faith available to a wider public, thus expanding university services beyond its own academic community.

37. In its service to society, a Catholic University *will relate especially to the academic, cultural, and scientific world* of the region in which it is located. Original forms of dialogue and collaboration are to be encouraged between the Catholic Universities and the other Universities of a nation on behalf of development, of understanding between cultures, and of the defense of nature in accordance with an awareness of the international ecological situation.

Catholic Universities join other private and public institutions in serving the public interest through higher education and research; they are one among the variety of different types of institutions that are necessary for the free expression of cultural diversity, and they are committed to the promotion of solidarity and its meaning in society and in the world. Therefore, they have the full right to expect that civil society and public authorities will recognize and defend their institutional autonomy and academic freedom; moreover, they have the right to the financial support that is necessary for their continued existence and development.

2. Pastoral Ministry

38. Pastoral ministry is that activity of the University which offers the members of the university community an opportunity to integrate religious and moral principles with their academic study and non-academic activities, *thus integrating faith with life.* It is part of the mission of the Church within the University, and is also a constitutive element of a Catholic University itself, both in its structure and in its life. A university community concerned with promoting the Institution's Catholic character will be conscious of this pastoral dimension and sensitive to the ways in which it can have an influence on all university activities.

39. As a natural expression of the Catholic identity of the University, the university community *should give a practical demonstration of its faith in its daily activity*, with important moments of reflection and of prayer. Catholic members of this community will be offered opportunities to assimilate Catholic teaching and practice into their lives and will be encouraged to participate in the celebration of the sacraments, especially the Eucharist as the most perfect act of community worship. When the academic community includes members of other Churches, ecclesial communities, or religions, their initiatives for reflection and prayer in accordance with their own beliefs are to be respected.

40. Those involved in pastoral ministry will encourage teachers and students to become more aware of their responsibility towards those who are suffering physically or spiritually. Following the example of Christ, they will be particularly attentive to the poorest and to those who suffer economic, social,

cultural or religious injustice. This responsibility begins within the academic community, but it also finds application beyond it.

41. Pastoral ministry is an indispensable means by which Catholic students can, in fulfillment of their baptism, *be prepared for active participation in the life of the Church*; it can assist in developing and nurturing the value of marriage and family life, fostering vocations to the priesthood and religious life, stimulating the Christian commitment of the laity and imbuing every activity with the spirit of the Gospel. Close cooperation between pastoral ministry in a Catholic University and the other activities within the local Church, under the guidance or with the approval of the diocesan Bishop, will contribute to their mutual growth.[35]

42. Various associations or movements of spiritual and apostolic life, especially those developed specifically for students, can be of great assistance in developing the pastoral aspects of university life.

3. Cultural Dialogue

43. By its very nature, a University develops culture through its research, helps to transmit the local culture to each succeeding generation through its teaching, and assists cultural activities through its educational services. It is open to all human experience and is ready to dialogue with and learn from any culture. A Catholic University shares in this, offering the rich experience of the Church's own culture. In addition, a Catholic University, aware that human culture is open to Revelation and transcendence, is also a primary and privileged place for a *fruitful dialogue between the Gospel and culture.*

44. Through this dialogue a Catholic University assists the Church, enabling it to come to a better knowledge of diverse cultures, discern their positive and negative aspects, to receive their authentically human contributions, and to develop means by which it can make the faith better understood by the men and women of a particular culture.[36] While it is true that the Gospel cannot be identified with any particular culture and transcends all cultures, it is also true that "the Kingdom which the Gospel proclaims is lived by men and women who are profoundly linked to a culture, and the building up of the Kingdom cannot avoid borrowing the elements of human culture or cultures."[37] "A faith that places itself on the margin of what is human, of what is therefore culture, would be a faith unfaithful to the fullness of what the Word of God manifests and reveals, a decapitated faith, worse still, a faith in the process of self-annihilation."[38]

45. A Catholic University must become *more attentive to the cultures of the world of today,* and to the *various cultural traditions existing within the*

Church in a way that will promote a continuous and profitable dialogue between the Gospel and modern society. Among the criteria that character-ize the values of a culture are above all, the *meaning of the human person*, his or her liberty, dignity, *sense of responsibility*, and openness to the transcendent. To a respect for persons is joined *the preeminent value of the family*, the primary unit of every human culture.

Catholic Universities will seek to discern and evaluate both the aspira-tions and the contradictions of modern culture, in order to make it more suited to the total development of individuals and peoples. In particular, it is recommended that by means of appropriate studies, the impact of modern technology and especially of the mass media on persons, the family, and the institutions and whole of modem culture be studied deeply. Traditional cul-tures are to be defended in their identity, helping them to receive modern values without sacrificing their own heritage, which is a wealth for the whole of the human family. Universities, situated within the ambience of these cul-tures, will seek to harmonize local cultures with the positive contributions of modern cultures.

46. An area that particularly interests a Catholic University is the *dia-logue between Christian thought and the modern sciences.* This task requires per-sons particularly well versed in the individual disciplines and who are at the same time adequately prepared theologically, and who are capable of con-fronting epistemological questions at the level of the relationship between faith and reason. Such dialogue concerns the natural sciences as much as the human sciences which posit new and complex philosophical and ethical problems. The Christian researcher should demonstrate the way in which human intelligence is enriched by the higher truth that comes from the Gospel: "The intelligence is never diminished, rather, it is stimulated and reinforced by that interior fount of deep understanding that is the Word of God, and by the hierarchy of values that results from it. . . . In its unique man-ner, the Catholic University helps to manifest the superiority of the spirit, that can never, without the risk of losing its very self, be placed at the service of something other than the search for truth."[39]

47. Besides cultural dialogue, a Catholic University, in accordance with its specific ends, and keeping in mind the various religious-cultural contexts, following the directives promulgated by competent ecclesiastical authority, can offer a contribution to ecumenical dialogue. It does so to further the search for unity among all Christians. In interreligious dialogue it will assist in discerning the spiritual values that are present in the different religions.

4. Evangelization

48. The primary mission of the Church is to preach the Gospel in such a way that a relationship between faith and life is established in each individual and in the socio-cultural context in which individuals live and act and communicate with one another. Evangelization means "bringing the Good News into all the strata of humanity, and through its influence transforming humanity from within and making it new. . . . It is a question not only of preaching the Gospel in ever wider geographic areas or to ever greater numbers of people, but also of affecting and, as it were, upsetting, through the power of the Gospel, humanity's criteria of judgment, determining values, points of interest, lines of thought, sources of inspiration, and models of life, which are in contrast with the Word of God and the plan of salvation."[40]

49. By its very nature, each Catholic University makes an important contribution to the Church's work of evangelization. It is a living *institutional* witness to Christ and his message, so vitally important in cultures marked by secularism, or where Christ and his message are still virtually unknown. Moreover, all the basic academic activities of a Catholic University are connected with and in harmony with the evangelizing mission of the Church: research carried out in the light of the Christian message which puts new human discoveries at the service of individuals and society; education offered in a faith-context that forms men and women capable of rational and critical judgment and conscious of the transcendent dignity of the human person; professional training that incorporates ethical values and a sense of service to individuals and to society; the dialogue with culture that makes the faith better understood, and the theological research that translates the faith into contemporary language. "Precisely because it is more and more conscious of its salvific mission in this world, the Church wants to have these centers closely connected with it; it wants to have them present and operative in spreading the authentic message of Christ."[41]

Part II
GENERAL NORMS
Article 1. The Nature of These Norms

§ 1. These General Norms are based on, and are a further development of, the *Code of Canon Law*[42] and the complementary Church legislation, without prejudice to the right of the Holy See to intervene should this become necessary. They are valid for all Catholic Universities and other Catholic Institutes of Higher Studies throughout the world.

§ 2. The General Norms are to be applied concretely at the local and regional levels by Episcopal Conferences and other Assemblies of Catholic Hierarchy[43] in conformity with the *Code of Canon Law* and complementary Church legislation, taking into account the Statutes of each University or Institute and, as far as possible and appropriate, civil law. After review by the Holy See,[44] these local or regional "Ordinances" will be valid for all Catholic Universities and other Catholic Institutes of Higher Studies in the region, except for Ecclesiastical Universities and Faculties. These latter Institutions, including Ecclesiastical Faculties which are part of a Catholic University, are governed by the norms of the Apostolic Constitution *Sapientia Christiana*.[45]

§ 3. A University established or approved by the Holy See, by an Episcopal Conference or another Assembly of Catholic Hierarchy, or by a diocesan Bishop is to incorporate these General Norms and their local and regional applications into its governing documents, and conform its existing Statutes both to the General Norms and to their applications, and submit them for approval to the competent ecclesiastical Authority. It is contemplated that other Catholic Universities, that is, those not established or approved in any of the above ways, with the agreement of the local ecclesiastical Authority, will make their own the General Norms and their local and regional applications, internalizing them into their governing documents, and, as far as possible, will conform their existing Statutes both to these General Norms and to their applications.

Article 2. The Nature of a Catholic University

§ 1. A Catholic University, like every university, is a community of scholars representing various branches of human knowledge. It is dedicated to research, to teaching, and to various kinds of service in accordance with its cultural mission.

§ 2. A Catholic University, as Catholic, informs and carries out its research, teaching, and all other activities with Catholic ideals, principles and attitudes. It is linked with the Church either by a formal, constitutive and statutory bond or by reason of an institutional commitment made by those responsible for it.

§ 3. Every Catholic University is to make known its Catholic identity, either in a mission statement or in some other appropriate public document, unless authorized otherwise by the competent ecclesiastical Authority. The University, particularly through its structure and its regulations, is to provide

means which will guarantee the expression and the preservation of this identity in a manner consistent with § 2.

§ 4. Catholic teaching and discipline are to influence all university
activities, while the freedom of conscience of each person is to be fully
respected.[46] Any official action or commitment of the University is to be in
accord with its Catholic identity.

§ 5. A Catholic University possesses the autonomy necessary to develop its
distinctive identity and pursue its proper mission. Freedom in research and
teaching is recognized and respected according to the principles and methods of
each individual discipline, so long as the rights of the individual and of the community are preserved within the confines of the truth and the common good.[47]

Article 3. The Establishment of a Catholic University

§ 1. A Catholic University may be established or approved by the Holy
See, by an Episcopal Conference or another Assembly of Catholic Hierarchy,
or by a diocesan Bishop.

§ 2. With the consent of the diocesan Bishop, a Catholic University may
also be established by a Religious Institute or other public juridical person.

§ 3. A Catholic University may also be established by other ecclesiastical or lay persons; such a University may refer to itself as a Catholic University only with the consent of the competent ecclesiastical Authority, in accordance with the conditions upon which both parties shall agree.[48]

§ 4. In the cases of §§ 1 and 2, the Statutes must be approved by the
competent ecclesiastical Authority.

Article 4. The University Community

§ 1. The responsibility for maintaining and strengthening the Catholic
identity of the University rests primarily with the University itself. While this
responsibility is entrusted principally to university authorities (including,
when the positions exist, the Chancellor and/or a Board of Trustees or equivalent body), it is shared in varying degrees by all members of the university
community, and therefore calls for the recruitment of adequate university
personnel, especially teachers and administrators, who are both willing and
able to promote that identity. The identity of a Catholic University is essentially linked to the quality of its teachers and to respect for Catholic doctrine.
It is the responsibility of the competent Authority to watch over these two
fundamental needs in accordance with what is indicated in Canon Law.[49]

§ 2. All teachers and all administrators, at the time of their appointment, are to be informed about the Catholic identity of the Institution and its implications, and about their responsibility to promote, or at least to respect, that identity.

§ 3. In ways appropriate to the different academic disciplines, all Catholic teachers are to be faithful to, and all other teachers are to respect, Catholic doctrine and morals in their research and teaching. In particular, Catholic theologians, aware that they fulfill a mandate received from the Church, are to be faithful to the Magisterium of the Church as the authentic interpreter of Sacred Scripture and Sacred Tradition.[50]

§ 4. Those university teachers and administrators who belong to other Churches, ecclesial communities, or religions, as well as those who profess no religious belief, and also all students, are to recognize and respect the distinctive Catholic identity of the University. In order not to endanger the Catholic identity of the University or Institute of Higher Studies, the number of non-Catholic teachers should not be allowed to constitute a majority within the Institution, which is and must remain Catholic.

§ 5. The education of students is to combine academic and professional development with formation in moral and religious principles and the social teachings of the Church; the program of studies for each of the various professions is to include an appropriate ethical formation in that profession. Courses in Catholic doctrine are to be made available to all students.[51]

Article 5. The Catholic University within the Church

§ 1. Every Catholic University is to maintain communion with the universal Church and the Holy See; it is to be in close communion with the local Church and in particular with the diocesan Bishops of the region or nation in which it is located. In ways consistent with its nature as a University, a Catholic University will contribute to the Church's work of evangelization.

§ 2. Each Bishop has a responsibility to promote the welfare of the Catholic Universities in his diocese and has the right and duty to watch over the preservation and strengthening of their Catholic character. If problems should arise concerning this Catholic character, the local Bishop is to take the initiatives necessary to resolve the matter, working with the competent university authorities in accordance with established procedures[52] and, if necessary, with the help of the Holy See.

§ 3. Periodically, each Catholic University, to which Article 3, 1, and 2 refers, is to communicate relevant information about the University and its activities to the competent ecclesiastical Authority. Other Catholic Universities are to communicate this information to the Bishop of the diocese in which the principal seat of the Institution is located.

Article 6. Pastoral Ministry

§ 1. A Catholic University is to promote the pastoral care of all members of the university community, and to be especially attentive to the spiritual development of those who are Catholics. Priority is to be given to those means which will facilitate the integration of human and professional education with religious values in the light of Catholic doctrine, in order to unite intellectual learning with the religious dimension of life.

§ 2. A sufficient number of qualified people—priests religious, and lay persons—are to be appointed to provide pastoral ministry for the university community, carried on in harmony and cooperation with the pastoral activities of the local Church under the guidance or with the approval of the diocesan Bishop. All members of the university community are to be invited to assist the work of pastoral ministry, and to collaborate in its activities.

Article 7. Cooperation

§ 1. In order better to confront the complex problems facing modern society, and in order to strengthen the Catholic identity of the Institutions, regional, national, and international cooperation is to be promoted in research, teaching, and other university activities among all Catholic Universities, including Ecclesiastical Universities and Faculties.[53] Such cooperation is also to be promoted between Catholic Universities and other Universities, and with other research and educational Institutions, both private and governmental.

§ 2. Catholic Universities will, when possible and in accord with Catholic principles and doctrine, cooperate with government programs and the programs of other national and international Organizations on behalf of justice, development, and progress.

TRANSITIONAL NORMS

Art. 8. The present Constitution will come into effect on the first day of the academic year 1991.

Art. 9. The application of the Constitution is committed to the Congregation for Catholic Education, which has the duty to promulgate the necessary directives that will serve towards that end.

Art. 10. It will be the competence of the Congregation for Catholic Education, when with the passage of time circumstances require it, to propose changes to be made in the present Constitution in order that it may be adapted continuously to the needs of Catholic Universities.

Art. 11. Any particular laws or customs presently in effect that are contrary to this Constitution are abolished. Also, any privileges granted up to this day by the Holy See whether to physical or moral persons that are contrary to this present Constitution are abolished.

Conclusion

The mission that the Church, with great hope, entrusts to Catholic Universities holds a cultural and religious meaning of vital importance because it concerns the very future of humanity. The renewal requested of Catholic Universities will make them better able to respond to the task of bringing the message of Christ to man, to society, to the various cultures: "Every human reality, both individual and social has been liberated by Christ: persons, as well as the activities of men and women, of which culture is the highest and incarnate expression. The salvific action of the Church on cultures is achieved, first of all, by means of persons, families, and educators . . . . Jesus Christ, our Savior, offers his light and his hope to all those who promote the sciences, the arts, letters, and the numerous fields developed by modern culture. Therefore, all the sons and daughters of the Church should become aware of their mission and discover how the strength of the Gospel can penetrate and regenerate the mentalities and dominant values that inspire individual cultures, as well as the opinions and mental attitudes that are derived from it."[54]

It is with fervent hope that I address this Document to all the men and women engaged in various ways in the significant mission of Catholic higher education.

Beloved Brothers and Sisters, my encouragement and my trust go with you in your weighty daily task that becomes ever more important, more urgent and necessary on behalf of Evangelization for the future of culture and of all cultures. The Church and the world have great need of your witness and of your capable, free, and responsible contribution.

Given in Rome, at Saint Peter's, on 15 August, the Solemnity of the Assumption of the Blessed Virgin Mary into Heaven, in the year 1990, the twelfth of the Pontificate.

NOTES

[1] Cf. the letter of Pope Alexander IV to the University of Paris, 14 April 1255, Introduction: *Bullarium Diplomatum . . .* , vol. III, Turin 1858, p. 602.

[2] SAINT AUGUSTINE, *Confes.* X, xxiii, 33: "In fact, the blessed life consists in *the joy that comes from the truth*, since this joy comes from You who are Truth, God my light, salvation of my face, my God." PL 32, 793-794. Cf. SAINT THOMAS AQUINAS, *De Malo*, IX, 1: "It is actually natural to man to strive for knowledge of the truth."

[3] JOHN PAUL II, Discourse to the "Institut Catholique de Paris," 1 June 1980: *Insegnamenti di Giovanni Paolo II*, Vol. III/1 (1980), p. 1581.

[4] JOHN PAUL II, Discourse to the Cardinals, 10 November 1979: *Insegnamenti di Giovanni Paolo II*, Vol. II/2 (1979), p. 1096; cf. Discourse to UNESCO, Paris, 2 June 1980: AAS 72 (1980), pp. 735-752.

[5] Cf. JOHN PAUL II, Discourse to the University of Coimbra, 15 May 1982: *Insegnamenti di Giovanni Paolo II*, Vol. V/2 (1982), p. 1692.

[6] PAUL VI, Allocution to Representatives of States, 4 October 1965: *Insegnamenti di Paolo VI*, Vol. III (1965), p. 508.

[7] JOHN HENRY CARDINAL NEWMAN, *The Idea of a University*, London, Longmans, Green and Company, 1931, p. XI.

[8] *Jn* 14:6.

[9] Cf. SAINT AUGUSTINE, Serm. 43, 9: PL 38, 258. Cf. also SAINT ANSELM, *Proslogion*, chap. I: PL 158, 227.

[10] Cf. JOHN PAUL II, Allocution to the International Congress on Catholic Universities, 25 April 1989, n. 3: AAS 18 (1989), p. 1218.

[11] JOHN PAUL II, Apostolic Constitution Sapientia Christiana concerning the Ecclesiastical Universities and Faculties, 15 April 1979: AAS 71 (1979), pp. 469-521.

[12] VATICAN COUNCIL II, Declaration on Catholic Education *Gravissimum Educationis*, n. 10: AAS 58 (1966), p. 737.

[13] *Mt* 13:52.

[14] Cf. *The Magna Carta of the European Universities*, Bologna, Italy, 18 September 1988, "Fundamental Principles."

[15] Cf. VATICAN COUNCIL II, Pastoral Constitution on the Church in the Modern World *Gaudium et Spes*, n. 59: AAS 58 (1966), p. 1080; Declaration on Catholic Education *Gravissimum Educationis*, n. 10: AAS 58 (1966), p. 737. "Institutional autonomy" means that the governance of an academic institution is and remains internal to the institution; "academic freedom" is the guarantee given to those involved in teaching and research that, within their specific specialized branch of knowledge, and according to the methods proper to that specific area, they may search for the truth wherever analysis and evidence leads them, and may teach and publish the results of this search, keeping in mind the cited criteria, that is, safeguarding the rights of the individual and of society within the confines of the truth and the common good.

[16] There is a two-fold notion of *culture* used in this document: the *humanistic* and the *socio-historical*. "The word 'culture' in its general sense indicates all those factors by which man refines and unfolds his manifold spiritual and bodily qualities. It means his effort to bring the world itself under his control by his knowledge and his labor. It includes the fact that by improving customs and institutions he renders social life more human both within the family and in the civic community. Finally, it is a feature of culture that throughout the course of time man expresses, communicates, and conserves in his works great spiritual experiences and desires, so that these may be of advantage to the progress of many, even of the whole human family. Hence it follows that human culture necessarily has a historical and social aspect and that the word 'culture' often takes on a sociological and ethnological sense." VATICAN COUNCIL II, Pastoral Constitution on the Church in the Modern World *Gaudium et Spes*, n. 53: AAS 58 (1966), p. 1075.

[17] *L'Université Catholique dans le monde moderne. Document final du 2ème Congrès des Délégués des Universités Catholiques*, Rome, 20-29 November 1972, § 1.

[18] *Ibid.*

[19] JOHN PAUL II, Allocution to the International Congress on Catholic Universities, 25 April 1989, n. 4: AAS 81 (1989), p. 1219. Cf. also VATICAN COUNCIL II, Pastoral Constitution

on the Church in the Modern World *Gaudium et Spes*, n. 61: AAS 58 (1966), pp. 1081-1082. Cardinal Newman observes that a University "professes to assign to each study which it receives, its proper place and its just boundaries; to define the rights, to establish the mutual relations, and to effect the intercommunion of one and all." (*Op. cit.*, p. 457).

[20] VATICAN COUNCIL II, Pastoral Constitution on the Church in the Modern World *Gaudium et Spes*, n. 36: AAS 58 (1966), p. 1054. To a group of scientists I pointed out that "while reason and faith surely represent two distinct orders of knowledge, each autonomous with regard to its own methods, the two must finally converge in the discovery of a single whole reality which has its origin in God." (JOHN PAUL II, *Address at the Meeting on Galileo*, 9 May 1983, n. 3: AAS 75 [1983], p. 690).

[21] JOHN PAUL II, Address at UNESCO, 2 June 1980, n. 22: AAS 72 (1980), p. 750. The last part of the quotation uses words directed to the Pontifical Academy of Sciences, 10 November 1979: *Insegnamenti di Giovanni Paolo II*, Vol. II/2 (1979), p. 1109.

[22] Cf. VATICAN COUNCIL II, Declaration on Catholic Education *Gravissimum Educationis*, n. 10: AAS 58 (1966), p. 737.

[23] VATICAN COUNCIL II, Pastoral Constitution on the Church in the Modern World *Gaudium et Spes*, n. 59: AAS 58 (1966), p. 1080. Cardinal Newman describes the ideal to be sought in this way: "A habit of mind is formed which lasts through life, of which the attributes are freedom, equitableness, calmness, moderation, and wisdom." (*Op. cit.*, pp. 101-102).

[24] JOHN PAUL II, Post-Synodal Apostolic Exhortation *Christifideles Laici*, 30 December 1988, n. 44: AAS 81 (1989), p. 479.

[25] VATICAN COUNCIL II, Dogmatic Constitution on the Church *Lumen Gentium*, n. 31: AAS 57 (1965), pp. 37-38. Cf. Decree on the Apostolate of the Laity *Apostolicam Actuositatem*, passim: AAS 58 (1966), pp. 837ff. Cf. also *Gaudium et Spes*, n. 43: AAS 58 (1966), pp. 1061-1064.

[26] Cf. VATICAN COUNCIL II, Declaration on Religious Liberty *Dignitatis Humanae*, n. 2: AAS 58 (1966), pp. 930-931.

[27] JOHN PAUL II, Address to Leaders of Catholic Higher Education, Xavier University of Louisiana, U.S.A., 12 September 1987, n. 4: AAS 80 (1988), p. 764.

[28] VATICAN COUNCIL II, Pastoral Constitution on the Church in the Modern World *Gaudium et Spes*, n. 59: AAS 58 (1966), p. 1080.

[29] Cf. VATICAN COUNCIL II, Dogmatic Constitution on Divine Revelation *Dei Verbum*, nn. 8-10: AAS 58 (1966), pp. 820-822.

[30] Cf. VATICAN COUNCIL II, Dogmatic Constitution on the Church *Lumen Gentium*, n. 25: AAS 57 (1965), pp. 29-31.

[31] Cf. "Instruction on the Ecclesial Vocation of the Theologian" of the Congregation for the Doctrine of the Faith of 24 May 1990.

[32] Cf. JOHN PAUL II, Encyclical Letter *Sollicitudo Rei Socialis*, nn. 27-34: AAS 80 (1988), pp. 547-560.

[33] PAUL VI, Encyclical Letter *Populorum Progressio*, n. 1: AAS 59 (1967), p. 257.

[34] "Therefore, in that there has been a pleasing multiplication of centers of higher learning, it has become apparent that it would be opportune for the faculty and the alumni to unite in common association which, working in reciprocal understanding and close collaboration, and based upon the authority of the Supreme Pontiff, as father and universal doctor, they might more efficaciously spread and extend the light of Christ." (Plus XII, Apostolic Letter *Catholicas Studiorum Universitates*, with which The International Federation of Catholic Universities was established: AAS 42 [1950], p. 386).

[35] The *Code of Canon Law* indicates the general responsibility of the Bishop toward university students: "The diocesan bishop is to have serious pastoral concern for students by erecting a parish for them or by assigning priests for this purpose on a stable basis; he is also to provide for Catholic university centers at universities, even non-Catholic ones, to give assistance, especially spiritual to young people." (*CIC*, can. 813).

[36] "Living in various circumstances during the course of time, the Church, too, has used in her preaching the discoveries of different cultures to spread and explain the message of Christ to all nations, to probe it and more deeply understand it, and to give it better expression in litur-

gical celebrations and in the life of the diversified community of the faithful." (VATICAN COUNCIL II, Pastoral Constitution on the Church in the Modern World *Gaudium et Spes*, n. 58: AAS 58 [1966], p. 1079).

[37] PAUL VI, Apostolic Exhortation *Evangelii Nuntiandi*, n. 20: AAS 68 (1976), p. 18. Cf. VATICAN COUNCIL II, Pastoral Constitution on the Church in the Modern World *Gaudium et Spes*, n. 58: AAS 58 (1966), p. 1079.

[38] JOHN PAUL II, Address to Intellectuals, to Students and to University Personnel at Medellín, Colombia, 5 July 1986, n. 3: AAS 79 (1987), p. 99. Cf. also VATICAN COUNCIL II, Pastoral Constitution on the Church in the Modern World *Gaudium et Spes*, n. 58: AAS 58 (1966), p. 1079.

[39] PAUL VI, to the Delegates of The International Federation of Catholic Universities, 27 November 1972: AAS 64 (1972), p. 770.

[40] PAUL VI, Apostolic Exhortation *Evangelii Nuntiandi*, nn. 18ff.: AAS 68 (1976), pp. 17-18.

[41] PAUL VI, Address to Presidents and Rectors of the Universities of the Society of Jesus, 6 August 1975, n. 2: AAS 67 (1975), p. 533. Speaking to the participants of the International Congress on Catholic Universities, 25 April 1989, I added (n. 5): "Within a Catholic University the evangelical mission of the Church and the mission of research and teaching become *interrelated* and *coordinated*": Cf. AAS 81 (1989), p. 1220.

[42] Cf. in particular the Chapter of the Code: "Catholic Universities and other Institutes of Higher Studies" (CIC, cann. 807-814).

[43] Episcopal Conferences were established in the Latin Rite. Other Rites have other Assemblies of Catholic Hierarchy.

[44] Cf. CIC, Can. 455, § 2.

[45] Cf. *Sapientia Christiana*: AAS 71 (1979), pp. 469-521. Ecclesiastical Universities and Faculties are those that have the right to confer academic degrees by the authority of the Holy See.

[46] Cf. VATICAN COUNCIL II, Declaration on Religious Liberty *Dignitatis Humanae*, n. 2: AAS 58 (1966), pp. 930-931.

[47] Cf. VATICAN COUNCIL II, Pastoral Constitution on the Church in the Modern World *Gaudium et Spes*, nn. 57 and 59: AAS 58 (1966), pp. 1077-1080; *Gravissimum Educationis*, n. 10: AAS 58 (1966), p. 737.

[48] Both the establishment of such a university and the conditions by which it may refer to itself as a Catholic University are to be in accordance with the prescriptions issued by the Holy See, Episcopal Conference or other Assembly of Catholic Hierarchy.

[49] Canon 810 of CIC specifies the responsibility of the competent Authorities in this area: § 1 "It is the responsibility of the authority who is competent in accord with the statutes to provide for the appointment of teachers to Catholic universities who, besides their scientific and pedagogical suitability, are also outstanding in their integrity of doctrine and probity of life; when those requisite qualities are lacking they are to be removed from their positions in accord with the procedure set forth in the statutes. § 2 The conference of bishops and the diocesan bishops concerned have the duty and right of being vigilant that in these universities the principles of Catholic doctrine are faithfully observed." Cf. also Article 5, 2 ahead in these "Norms."

[50] VATICAN COUNCIL II, Dogmatic Constitution on the Church *Lumen Gentium*, n. 25: AAS 57 (1965), p. 29; *Dei Verbum*, nn. 8-10: AAS 58 (1966), pp. 820-822; Cf. CIC, can. 812: "It is necessary that those who teach theological disciplines in any institute of higher studies have a mandate from the competent ecclesiastical authority."

[51] Cf. CIC, can 811 § 2.

[52] For Universities to which Article 3 §§ 1 and 2 refer, these procedures are to be established in the university statutes approved by the competent ecclesiastical Authority; for other Catholic Universities, they are to be determined by Episcopal Conferences or other Assemblies of Catholic Hierarchy.

[53] Cf. CIC, can. 820. Cf. also *Sapientia Christiana*, Norms of Application, Article 49: AAS 71 (1979), p. 512.

[54] JOHN PAUL II, to the Pontifical Council for Culture, 13 January 1989, n. 2: AAS 81 (1989), pp. 857-858.

The Application of
Ex corde Ecclesiae
for the United States

In November 1999, Most Reverend Joseph A. Fiorenza, president of the National Conference of Catholic Bishops, petitioned the Apostolic See that these executive norms of the apostolic constitution *Ex corde Ecclesiae*, approved according to the norm of law by a plenary session of the Conference, be duly granted recognition. In May 2000, the Congregation for Bishops, after consultation with the Congregation for Catholic Education and the Pontifical Council for the Interpretation of Legislative Texts, found these norms in conformity with universal canon law and declared them valid. These norms are printed here as *The Application of Ex corde Ecclesiae for the United States*, which is authorized for publication by the undersigned.

> Monsignor Dennis M. Schnurr
> General Secretary
> NCCB/USCC

Decree of Promulgation

On November 17, 1999, the Catholic Bishops of the United States, meeting in Plenary Session of the National Conference of Catholic Bishops, approved *The Application of Ex corde Ecclesiae for the United States* implementing the Apostolic Constitution *Ex corde Ecclesiae*, according to the norm of law.

The action was granted *recognitio* by the Congregation for Bishops in accord with article 82 of the Apostolic Constitution *Pastor Bonus* and issued by Decree of the Congregation for Bishops signed by His Eminence Lucas Cardinal Moreira Neves, Prefect, and His Excellency Most Reverend Francisco Monterisi, Secretary, and dated May 3, 2000.

The Application of "Ex corde Ecclesiae" for the United States. Washington, DC: United States Conference of Catholic Bishops, 2000.

75

As President of the National Conference of Catholic Bishops, I hereby decree that *The Application of Ex corde Ecclesiae for the United States* will be in force as particular law for the United States on May 3, 2001.

Given at the offices of the National Conference of Catholic Bishops in Washington, DC, on June 1, 2000.

> Most Reverend Joseph A. Fiorenza
> Bishop of Galveston-Houston
> President, National Conference of Catholic Bishops

Introduction

Catholic higher education in the United States has a unique history. The opening of Georgetown in 1789 and subsequent growth into 230 Catholic colleges and universities is a remarkable achievement for the Church and the United States.

Catholic colleges and universities are related to the ecclesial community, to the higher education enterprise of the United States and to the broader society. Founded and developed principally by religious communities of women and men, they now involve lay administrators, professors and trustees who are Catholic and not Catholic—all committed to the vision of Catholic higher education.

Catholic colleges and universities, where culture and faith intersect, bring diversity to American higher education. Diversity is present among the institutions themselves: two-year colleges and graduate program universities; liberal arts colleges and research universities; schools for the professions and schools for technical education.

To all participating in Catholic higher education, the Bishops of the United States express their admiration and sincere gratitude, knowing that both the nation and ecclesial community are affected by their commitments and talents. Bishops want to maintain, preserve and guarantee the Catholic identity of Catholic higher education, a responsibility they share in various ways with sponsoring religious communities, boards of trustees, university administration, faculty, staff and students.

Part One
THEOLOGICAL AND PASTORAL PRINCIPLES

1. *Ex corde Ecclesiae*

On August 15, 1990, Pope John Paul II issued an apostolic constitution on Catholic higher education entitled *Ex corde Ecclesiae*.[1] The Apostolic Constitution described the identity and mission of Catholic colleges and universities and provided General Norms to help fulfill its vision.

The General Norms are to be applied concretely by episcopal conferences, taking into account the status of each college and university and, as far as possible and appropriate, civil law. Accordingly, recognizing that the Apostolic Constitution *Ex corde Ecclesiae* is normative for the Church throughout the world, this document seeks to apply its principles and norms to all Catholic colleges, universities, and institutions of higher learning within the territory encompassed by the United States Catholic Conference of Bishops.

2. The Ecclesiological Concept of Communion

The Church is made up of individual faithful and communities linked with one another through many active ecclesial relationships. A true understanding of these dynamic relationships flows from the faith-conviction that God the Father, through His incarnate Son, Jesus Christ, has revealed His desire to incorporate all people into the life of the Trinity. It is in the Church, through the indwelling of the Holy Spirit, that this relationship of all persons and communities with the Triune God takes place. This body of dynamic relationships held together by the unity of faith is aptly described in the theological concept of communion.[2]

The dynamic of communion unites on a deeper and more productive level the various communities in the Church through which so much of her mission of salvation, and consequently human progress, is carried out. More specifically, ecclesial communion furnishes the basis for the collaborative relationships between the hierarchy and Catholic universities contemplated in *Ex corde Ecclesiae*: "Every Catholic University is to maintain communion with the universal Church and the Holy See; it is to be in close communion with the local Church and in particular with the diocesan bishops of the region or the nation in which it is located."[3] The Catholic university is a vital institution in the communion of the Church and is "a primary and privileged place for a fruitful dialogue between the Gospel and culture."[4]

The richness of communion illuminates the ecclesial relationship that unites the distinct, and yet complementary, teaching roles of bishops and Catholic universities. In the light of communion, the teaching responsibilities of the hierarchy and of the Catholic universities retain their distinctive autonomous nature and goal but are joined as complementary activities contributing to the fulfillment of the Church's universal teaching mission. The communion of the Church embraces both the pastoral work of bishops and the academic work of Catholic universities, thus linking the bishops' right and obligation to communicate and safeguard the integrity of Church doctrine with the right and obligation of Catholic universities to investigate, analyze and communicate all truth freely.

The communion of all the faithful with the Triune God and with one another is a theological reality expressing the will of God. It is by understanding and living this communion that bishops and Catholic universities can most effectively collaborate to fulfill their proper mission within the Church. In carrying out its mission to search for truth, the Catholic university is uniquely situated to serve not only the people of God but the entire human family "in their pilgrimage to the transcendent goal which gives meaning to life."[5]

3. The Catholic University's Twofold Relationship

Catholic universities are participants in the life of the universal Church, the local Church, the higher education community of the United States and the civic community. As such, they "are called to continuous renewal, both as 'universities' and as 'Catholic.'"[6] This twofold relationship is described in the May 22, 1994, joint document of the Congregation for Catholic Education and the Pontifical Councils for the Laity and for Culture, which states that the Catholic university achieves its purpose when

> . . . it gives proof of being rigorously serious as a member of the international community of knowledge and expresses its Catholic identity through an explicit link with the Church, at both local and universal levels—an identity which marks concretely the life, the services and the programs of the university community. In this way, by its very existence, the Catholic university achieves its aim of guaranteeing, in institutional form, a Christian presence in the university world. . . .[7]

One of the ways this relationship is clarified and maintained is through dialogue that includes faculty of all disciplines, students, staff, academic and other administrative officers, trustees, and sponsoring religious communities of the educational institutions, all of whom share responsibility for the character of Catholic higher education. The bishop and his collaborators in the local Church are integral parties in this dialogue.

The Catholic university is related to the local and universal ecclesial community[8] as well as to the broader society[9] and the higher education academy.[10] In this document we are directing special attention to the relationship between universities and Church authorities. *Ex corde Ecclesiae* provides one of the ecclesiological principles to address this specific relationship.

> Bishops have a particular responsibility to promote Catholic Universities, and especially to promote and assist in the preservation and strengthening of their Catholic identity, including the protection of their Catholic identity in relation to civil authorities. This will be achieved more effectively if close personal and pastoral relationships exist between University and Church authorities, characterized by *mutual trust, close and consistent cooperation and continuing dialogue*. Even though they do not enter directly into the internal government of the University, Bishops "should be seen not as external agents but as participants in the life of the Catholic University." [italics added][11]

Each of these elements in the pastoral relationship of bishops with Catholic universities warrants attention.

4. Mutual Trust Between University and Church Authorities

Mutual trust goes beyond the personalities of those involved in the relationship. The trust is grounded in a shared baptismal belief in the truths that are rooted in Scripture and Tradition, as interpreted by the Church, concerning the mystery of the Trinity: God the Father and Creator, who works even until now; God the Son and incarnate Redeemer, who is the Way and the Truth and the Life; and God the Holy Spirit, the Paraclete, whom the Father and Son send. In the spirit of *communio*, the relationship of trust between university and Church authorities, based on these shared beliefs with their secular and religious implications, is fostered by mutual listening, by collaboration that respects differing responsibilities and gifts, and by a solidarity that mutually recognizes respective statutory limitations and responsibilities.

5. Close and Consistent Cooperation Between University and Church Authorities

Collaborating to integrate faith with life is a necessary part of the "close personal and pastoral relationships"[12] to which universities and bishops are called. Within their academic mission of teaching and research, in ways appropriate to their own constituencies and histories, including their sponsorship by religious communities, institutions offer courses in Catholic theology that reflect current scholarship and are in accord with the authentic teaching of the Church.

Many cooperative programs, related to Gospel outreach, already flourish throughout the country. It is highly desirable that representatives of both educational institutions and Church authorities jointly identify, study, and pursue solutions to issues concerning social justice, human life and the needs of the poor.

Allocation of personnel and money to assure the special contributions of campus ministry is indispensable. In view of the presence on campus of persons of other religious traditions, it is a concern of the whole Church that ecumenical and inter-religious relationships should be fostered with sensitivity.

A structure and strategy to insure ongoing dialogue and cooperation should be established by university and Church authorities.

6. Continuing Dialogue Among University Representatives and Church Authorities

Dialogues occasioned by *Ex corde Ecclesiae* may be graced moments characterized by

a. a manifest openness to a further analysis and local appropriation of Catholic identity;

b. an appreciation of the positive contributions that campus-wide conversations make; and

c. a conviction that conversation can develop and sustain relationships.

A need exists for continued attention and commitment to the far-reaching implications—curricular, staffing, programming—of major themes within *Ex corde Ecclesiae*. These include Catholic identity, *communio*, relating faith and culture, pastoral outreach, the New Evangelization, and relationship to the Church.

7. Catholic Identity

Catholic identity lies at the heart of *Ex corde Ecclesiae*. In 1979, Pope John Paul II, in an address to the Catholic academic community at The Catholic University of America, stressed the importance of the Catholic character of Catholic institutions of higher learning:

> Every university or college is qualified by a specified mode of being.
> Yours is the qualification of being Catholic, of affirming God, his reve-

lation and the Catholic Church as the guardian and interpreter of that revelation. The term 'Catholic' will never be a mere label either added or dropped according to the pressures of varying factors.[13]

Catholic universities, in addition to their academic commitments to secular goals and programs, should excel in theological education, prayer and liturgy, and works of charity. These religious activities, however, do not alone make a university "Catholic." *Ex corde Ecclesiae* highlights four distinctive characteristics that are essential for Catholic identity:

   a. Christian inspiration in individuals and the university community;

   b. Reflection and research on human knowledge in the light of the Catholic faith;

   c. Fidelity to the Christian message in conformity with the magisterium of the Church;

   d. Institutional commitment to the service of others.[14]

Catholic universities cherish their Catholic tradition and, in many cases, the special charisms of the religious communities that founded them. In the United States, they enjoyed the freedom to incorporate these religious values into their academic mission. The principles of *Ex corde Ecclesiae* afford them an opportunity to re-examine their origin and renew their way of living out this precious heritage.

Catholic universities enjoy institutional autonomy: as academic institutions their governance "is and remains internal to the institution."[15] In order to maintain and safeguard their freely-chosen Catholic identity, it is important for Catholic universities to set out clearly in their official documentation their Catholic character and to implement in practical terms their commitment to the essential elements of Catholic identity, including the following:

   e. Commitment to be faithful to the teachings of the Catholic Church;

   f. Commitment to Catholic ideals, principles and attitudes in carrying out research, teaching and all other university activities, including activities of officially-recognized student and faculty organizations and associations, and with due regard for academic freedom and the conscience of every individual;[16]

   g. Commitment to serve others, particularly the poor, underprivileged and vulnerable members of society;

   h. Commitment of witness of the Catholic faith by Catholic administrators and teachers, especially those teaching the theological disciplines, and acknowledgment and respect on the part of non-Catholic teachers and administrators of the university's Catholic identity and mission;

i. Commitment to provide courses for students on Catholic moral and religious principles and their application to critical areas such as human life and other issues of social justice;

j. Commitment to care pastorally for the students, faculty, administration and staff;

k. Commitment to provide personal services (health care, counseling and guidance) to students, as well as administration and faculty, in conformity with the Church's ethical and religious teaching and directives; and

l. Commitment to create a campus culture and environment that is expressive and supportive of a Catholic way of life.

Catholic universities should make every effort to enhance their communion with the hierarchy so that through this special relationship they may assist each other to accomplish the mission to which they are mutually committed.

In a secular world the strong Catholic identity of our institutes of higher learning is invaluable in witnessing to the relationship of truth and reason, the call of the revealed Word, and the authentic meaning of human life. "The present age is in urgent need of this kind of disinterested service, namely of proclaiming the meaning of truth, that fundamental value without which freedom, justice and human dignity are extinguished."[17]

Part Two
PARTICULAR NORMS

The chief purpose of the following norms is to assist Catholic colleges and universities in their internal process of reviewing their Catholic identity and clarifying their essential mission and goals. They are intended to provide practical guidance to those committed to the enterprise of Catholic higher education as they seek to implement the theological and pastoral principles of Ex corde Ecclesiae. Accordingly, the norms follow the basic outline of the General Norms found in Ex corde Ecclesiae and provide concrete steps that will facilitate the implementation of the Holy Father's document in the context of the relevant sections of the Code of Canon Law and complementary Church legislation.[18]

ART. 1. The Nature of the Particular Norms

1. These particular norms are applicable to all Catholic colleges, universities and institutions of higher learning within the territory encompassed by the National Conference of Catholic Bishops, contrary particular laws, customs or privileges notwithstanding.[19]

2. Catholic universities are to observe the general norms of *Ex corde Ecclesiae* and the following particular norms as they apply to their individual institutions, taking into account their own statutes and, as far as possible and appropriate, relevant provisions of applicable federal and state law, regulations and procedures.

> a. Those universities established or approved by the Holy See, by the NCCB, by other hierarchical assemblies, or by individual diocesan bishops are to incorporate, by reference and in other appropriate ways, the general and particular norms into their governing documents and conform their existing statutes to such norms. Within five years of the effective date of these particular norms, Catholic universities are to submit the aforesaid incorporation for review and affirmation to the university's competent ecclesiastical authority.

> b. Other Catholic universities are to make the general and particular norms their own, include them in the university's official documentation by reference and in other appropriate ways, and, as much as possible, conform their existing statutes to such norms. These steps to ensure their Catholic identity are to be carried out in agreement with the diocesan bishop of the place where the seat of the university is situated.[20]

> c. Changes in statutes of universities established by the hierarchy, religious institutes or other public juridic persons that substantially affect the nature, mission or Catholic identity of the university require the approval of competent ecclesiastical authority.[21]

3. Those establishing or sponsoring a Catholic university have an obligation to make certain that they will be able to carry out their canonical duties in a way acceptable under relevant provisions of applicable federal and state law, regulations and procedures.[22]

ART. 2. The Nature of a Catholic University

1. The purpose of a Catholic university is education and academic research proper to the disciplines of the university. Since it enjoys the institutional autonomy appropriate to an academic institution, its governance is and remains internal to the institution itself. This fundamental purpose and

institutional autonomy must be respected and promoted by all, so that the university may effectively carry out its mission of freely searching for all truth.[23]

2. Academic freedom is an essential component of a Catholic university. The university should take steps to ensure that all professors are accorded "a lawful freedom of inquiry and of thought, and of freedom to express their minds humbly and courageously about those matters in which they enjoy competence."[24] In particular, "[t]hose who are engaged in the sacred disciplines enjoy a lawful freedom of inquiry and of prudently expressing their opinions on matters in which they have expertise, while observing the submission [*obsequio*] due to the magisterium of the Church."[25]

3. With due regard for the common good and the need to safeguard and promote the integrity and unity of the faith, the diocesan bishop has the duty to recognize and promote the rightful academic freedom of professors in Catholic universities in their search for truth.[26]

4. Recognizing the dignity of the human person, a Catholic university, in promoting its own Catholic identity and fostering Catholic teaching and discipline, must respect the religious liberty of every individual, a right with which each is endowed by nature.[27]

5. A responsibility of every Catholic university is to affirm its essential characteristics, in accord with the principles of *Ex corde Ecclesiae*, through public acknowledgment in its mission statement and/or its other official documentation of its canonical status[28] and its commitment to the practical implications of its Catholic identity, including but not limited to those specified in Part One, Section 7 of this document.

6. The university (in particular, the trustees, administration, and faculty) should take practical steps to implement its mission statement in order to foster and strengthen its Catholic nature and character.[29]

ART. 3. The Establishment of a Catholic University

1. A Catholic university may be established, or an existing university approved, by the Holy See, the National Conference of Catholic Bishops, other hierarchical assemblies, or individual diocesan bishops. It may also be established by a religious institute or some other public juridic person, or by individual Catholics, acting singly or in association, with proper ecclesiastical approval.[30]

2. At the time of its establishment the university should see to it that its canonical status is identified, including the ecclesiastical authority by which it has been established or approved or to which it otherwise relates.[31]

3. The statutes of Catholic universities established by hierarchical authority or by religious institutes or other public juridic persons must be approved by competent ecclesiastical authority.[32]

4. No university may assume the title Catholic without the consent of the competent ecclesiastical authority.[33]

ART. 4. The University Community

1. The responsibility for safeguarding and strengthening the Catholic identity of the university rests primarily with the university itself. All the members of the university community are called to participate in this important task in accordance with their specific roles: the sponsoring religious community, the board of trustees, the administration and staff, the faculty, and the students.[34] Men and women of religious faiths other than Catholic, on the board of trustees, on the faculty, and in other positions, can make a valuable contribution to the university. Their presence affords the opportunity for all to learn and benefit from each other. The university should welcome them as full partners in the campus community.

2. *The Board of Trustees*

a. Each member of the board must be committed to the practical implications of the university's Catholic identity as set forth in its mission statement or equivalent document.

b. To the extent possible, the majority of the board should be Catholics committed to the Church.

c. The board should develop effective ways of relating to and collaborating with the local bishop and diocesan agencies on matters of mutual concern.[35]

d. The board should analyze ecclesiastical documents on higher education, such as *Ex corde Ecclesiae* and this Application, and develop specific ways of implementing them appropriate to the structure and life of the university.

e. The board should see to it that the university periodically undertakes an internal review of the congruence of its mission statement, its courses of instruction, its research program, and its service activity with the ideals, principles and norms expressed in *Ex corde Ecclesiae*.

3. *Administration and Staff*

a. The university president should be a Catholic.[36]

b. The administration should inform faculty and staff at the time of their appointment regarding the Catholic identity, mission and religious practices of the university and encourage them to participate, to the degree possible, in the spiritual life of the university.

c. The administration should be in dialogue with the local bishop about ways of promoting Catholic identity and the contribution that the university can make to the life of the Church in the area.

4. *Faculty*

a. In accordance with its procedures for the hiring and retention of professionally qualified faculty and relevant provisions of applicable federal and state law, regulations and procedures, the university should strive to recruit and appoint Catholics as professors so that, to the extent possible, those committed to the witness of the faith will constitute a majority of the faculty. All professors are expected to be aware of and committed to the Catholic mission and identity of their institutions.

b. All professors are expected to exhibit not only academic competence and good character but also respect for Catholic doctrine.[37] When these qualities are found to be lacking, the university statutes are to specify the competent authority and the process to be followed to remedy the situation.[38]

c. Catholic theology should be taught in every Catholic university, and, if possible, a department or chair of Catholic theology should be established. Academic events should be organized on a regular basis to address theological issues, especially those relative to the various disciplines taught in the university.[39]

d. Both the university and the bishops, aware of the contributions made by theologians to Church and academy, have a right to expect them to present authentic Catholic teaching. Catholic professors of the theological disciplines have a corresponding duty to be faithful to the Church's magisterium as the authoritative interpreter of Sacred Scripture and Sacred Tradition.

e. Catholics who teach the theological disciplines in a Catholic university are required to have a *mandatum* granted by competent ecclesiastical authority.[40]

i. The *mandatum* is fundamentally an acknowledgment by Church authority that a Catholic professor of a theological discipline is a teacher within the full communion of the Catholic Church.

ii. The *mandatum* should not be construed as an appointment, authorization, delegation or approbation of one's teaching by Church authorities. Those who have received a *mandatum* teach in their own name in virtue of their baptism and their academic and professional competence, not in the name of the Bishop or of the Church's magisterium.[41]

iii. The *mandatum* recognizes the professor's commitment and responsibility to teach authentic Catholic doctrine and to refrain from putting forth as Catholic teaching anything contrary to the Church's magisterium.

iv. The following procedure is given to facilitate, as of the effective date of this Application, the process of requesting and granting the *mandatum*. Following the approval of the Application, a detailed procedure will be developed outlining the process of requesting and granting (or withdrawing) the *mandatum*.

(1) The competent ecclesiastical authority to grant the *mandatum* is the bishop of the diocese in which the Catholic university is located; he may grant the *mandatum* personally or through a delegate.[42]

(2) Without prejudice to the rights of the local bishop,[43] a *mandatum*, once granted, remains in effect wherever and as long as the professor teaches unless and until withdrawn by competent ecclesiastical authority.

(3) The *mandatum* should be given in writing. The reasons for denying or removing a *mandatum* should also be in writing.[44]

5. *Students.* With due regard for the principles of religious liberty and freedom of conscience, students should have the opportunity to be educated in the Church's moral and religious principles and social teachings and to participate in the life of faith.[45]

a. Catholic students have a right to receive from a university instruction in authentic Catholic doctrine and practice, especially from those who teach the theological disciplines. They also have a right to be provided with opportunities to practice the faith through participation in Mass, the sacraments, religious devotions and other authentic forms of Catholic spirituality.

b. Courses in Catholic doctrine and practice should be made available to all students.

c. Catholic teaching should have a place, if appropriate to the subject matter, in the various disciplines taught in the university.[46] Students should be provided with adequate instruction on professional ethics and moral issues related to their profession and the secular disciplines.

ART. 5. The Catholic University in the Church

1. The Universal Church

a. The university shall develop and maintain a plan for fulfilling its mission that communicates and develops the Catholic intellectual tradition, is of service to the Church and society, and encourages the members of the university community to grow in the practice of the faith.[47]

b. The university plan should address intellectual and pastoral contributions to the mission of communicating Gospel values,[48] service to the poor, social justice initiatives, and ecumenical and inter-religious activities.

2. The Local Church

a. In accordance with Church teaching and the universal law of the Church, the local Bishop has a responsibility to promote the welfare of the Catholic universities in his diocese and to watch over the preservation and strengthening of their Catholic character.[49]

b. Bishops should, when appropriate, acknowledge publicly the service of Catholic universities to the Church and support the institution's Catholic identity if it is unjustifiably challenged.

c. Diocesan and university authorities should commit themselves mutually to regular dialogues to achieve the goals of Ex corde Ecclesiae according to local needs and circumstances.

d. University authorities and the local diocesan bishop should develop practical methods of collaboration that are harmonious with the university's structure and statutes. Similar forms of collaboration should also exist between the university and the religious institute to which it is related by establishment or tradition.[50]

e. Doctrinal Responsibilities: Approaches to Promoting Cooperation and Resolving Misunderstandings between Bishops and Theologians, approved and published by the National Conference of Catholic Bishops, June 17, 1989, can serve as a useful guide for diocesan bishops, professors of the theological disciplines and administrators of universities to promote informal cooperation and collaboration in the Church's teaching mission and the faithful observance within Catholic universities of the principles of Catholic doctrine.

f. Disputes about Church doctrine should be resolved, whenever possible, in an informal manner. At times, the resolution of such matters may benefit from formal doctrinal dialogue as proposed by *Doctrinal Responsibilities* and adapted by the parties in question.[51]

g. The National Conference of Catholic Bishops, through an appropriate committee structure, should continue to dialogue and collaborate with the Catholic academic community and its representative associations about ways of safeguarding and promoting the ideals, principles and norms expressed in *Ex corde Ecclesiae*.

ART. 6. Pastoral Ministry

1. The diocesan bishop has overall responsibility for the pastoral care of the university's students, faculty, administration and staff.[52]

2. The university, in cooperation with the diocesan bishop, shall make provision for effective campus ministry programs, including the celebration of the sacraments, especially the Eucharist and penance, other liturgical celebrations, and opportunities for prayer and spiritual reflection.[53]

3. When selecting pastoral ministers—priests, deacons, religious and lay persons—to carry on the work of campus ministry, the university authorities should work closely with the diocesan bishop and interested religious institutes. Without prejudice to the provision of canon 969, §2, priests and deacons must enjoy pastoral faculties from the local ordinary in order to exercise their ministry on campus.

4. With due regard for religious liberty and freedom of conscience, the university, in cooperation with the diocesan bishop, should collaborate in ecumenical and interfaith efforts to care for the pastoral needs of students, faculty and other university personnel who are not Catholic.

5. In these pastoral efforts, the university and the diocesan bishop should take account of the prescriptions and recommendations issued by the Holy See and the guidance and pastoral statements of the National Conference of Catholic Bishops.[54]

ART. 7. Cooperation

1. Catholic universities should commit themselves to cooperate in a special way with other Catholic universities, institutions and professional associations, in the United States and abroad, in order to build up the entire Catholic academic community.[55]

2. In collaborating with governmental agencies, regional associations, and other universities, whether public or private, Catholic universities should give corporate witness to and promote the Church's social teaching and its moral principles in areas such as the fostering of peace and justice, respect for all human life, the eradication of poverty and unjust discrimination, the development of all peoples and the growth of human culture.[56]

CONCLUSION

This Application will become effective one year after its *recognitio* by the Holy See.

During the five years following the effective date of this Application, the National Conference of Catholic Bishops in collaboration with representatives of Catholic universities should develop a mutually agreeable process to review and evaluate the implementation of *Ex corde Ecclesiae* and this Application, particularly regarding the nature, mission and Catholic identity of the universities.

Ten years after the effective date of this Application, the National Conference of Catholic Bishops will review this Application of *Ex corde Ecclesiae* for the United States.

The Bishops of the United States, in offering this application of *Ex corde Ecclesiae*, join in sentiments expressed by Pope John Paul II:

> I turn to the whole Church, convinced that Catholic universities are essential to her growth and to the development of Christian culture and human progress. For this reason, the entire ecclesial community is invited to give its support to Catholic institutions of higher education and to assist them in their process of development and renewal. . . .[57]

NOTES

[1] Pope John Paul II, Apostolic Constitution on Catholic Universities *Ex corde Ecclesiae*, August 15, 1990, AAS 82 (1990) pp. 1475-1509 [cited throughout the remainder of this document as *ECE*]. English translation: *Origins*, CNS Documentary Service, October 4, 1990. In accordance with canon 455, §1, the United States Conference of Bishops promulgates this Application as a response to the special mandate of the Apostolic See (cf. *ECE*, II, Art. 1, §2). The Application refers to Catholic universities and other institutes of higher learning (cf. canons 807-814); excluded from the Application's treatment are ecclesiastical universities and facul-

ties (cf. canons 815-821), which are governed by the Apostolic Constitution, *Sapientia Christiana* (*see below* footnote 19).

2 *See* Vatican Council II, Dogmatic Constitution on the Church (*Lumen Gentium*) 4, 7, 9-29 (Chapter II: the People of God) and *passim*; Congregation for the Doctrine of the Faith, "Letter to the Bishops of the Catholic Church on Some Aspects of the Church Understood as Communion," *Origins* 22 (1992), 108-112; *Catechism of the Catholic Church*, nn. 787-801 and *passim*; 1985 Extraordinary Synod of Bishops, "A Message to the People of God," *Origins* 15 (1985), 441-444, and "The Final Report," *Origins* 15 (1985), 444-450.

3 *ECE*, II, Art. 5, §1.

4 *ECE*, I, n. 43. *See also ECE*, I, n. 49. For purposes of stylistic simplicity, this document, in both the "Theological and Pastoral Principles" and "Particular Norms," uses the word "university" as a generic term to include universities, colleges and other institutions of higher learning.

5 *ECE*, I, 13, quoting from "The Catholic University in the Modern World," the final document of the Second International Congress of Delegates of Catholic Universities, Rome, November 20-29, 1972, Sec. 1.

6 *ECE*, Introduction, n. 7.

7 "The Church's Presence in the University and in University Culture," II, §2, *Origins*, June 16, 1994, 74-80.

8 *ECE*, I, nn. 27-29, 31.

9 *Ibid.*, I, nn. 32-37.

10 *Ibid.*, I, nn. 12, 37; II, Art. 7, §§1-2.

11 *Ibid.*, I, n. 28. The citation at the end is from John Paul II, *Address to Leaders of Catholic Higher Education*, Xavier University of Louisiana, U.S.A., September 12, 1987, n. 4: AAS 80 (1988) 764.

12 *ECE*, I, n. 28.

13 Pope John Paul II, *Address* "Ad prope et exstantes sedes Studiorum Universitatis Catholicae profectus hanc allocutionem fecit ad moderatores et doctores eiusdem Athenaei atque ad legatos Collegiorum Universitatumque Catholicarum totius Nationis," October 6, 1979, AAS 71:13 (1979) 1260.

14 *ECE*, I, n. 13 [quoting "The Catholic University in the Modern World," the final document of the Second International Congress of Delegates of Catholic Universities, Rome, November 20-29, 1972, Sec. 1].

15 *See ECE*, I, n. 12 and footnote 15; Vatican Council II, *Pastoral Constitution on the Church in the Modern World* (*Gaudium et Spes*) 59; *Declaration on Catholic Education* (*Gravissimum educationis*) 10.

16 *See ECE*, II, Art. 2, §§4-5.

17 *ECE*, I, n. 4.

18 *See ECE*, II, Art. 1, §§1 & 2.

19 *ECE*, II, Art. 11: "Any particular laws or customs presently in effect that are contrary to this constitution are abolished. Also, any privileges granted up to this day by the Holy See whether to physical or moral persons that are contrary to this present constitution are abolished." These Particular Norms are not applicable to ecclesiastical universities and faculties insofar as they are governed by the Apostolic Constitution *Sapientia Christiana*.

20 *See ECE*, II, Art. 1, §3.

21 *See ECE*, II, Art. 3, §4.

22 *See* canon 807 and *ECE*, Art. 3; Congregation for Catholic Education, *Directives to Assist in the Formulation of the Ordinances for the Apostolic Constitution* "Ex corde Ecclesiae," not dated, n. B1.

23 *See above* footnote 15.

24 Vatican Council II, Pastoral Constitution on the Church in the Modern World (*Gaudium et Spes*) 62. A university's commitment to Catholic ideals, principles and attitudes is not only consistent with academic freedom and the integrity of secular subjects, it requires "[f]reedom in research and teaching" and respect for "the principles and methods of each individual discipline." *ECE*, II, Art. 2, §5.

[25] C. 218.

[26] *See ECE*, II, Art. 2, §5.

[27] Though thoroughly imbued with Christian inspiration, the university's Catholic identity should in no way be construed as an excuse for religious indoctrination or proselytization. *See* Vatican Council II, Declaration on Religious Liberty (*Dignitatis humanae*) 2-4.

[28] *See* footnote 31 for a listing of canonical categories.

[29] In this regard, the university may wish to establish a "mission effectiveness committee" or some other appropriate structure to develop methods by which Catholics may promote the university's Catholic identity and those who are not Catholic may acknowledge and respect this identity.

[30] *ECE*, II, Art. 3, §§1-3, cf. Canon 808. Note that, under Canon 322, private associations of the faithful can acquire juridic personality by the issuance of a formal decree of competent ecclesiastical authority (§1) and approval of their statutes, retaining, all the while, their private character (§2).

[31] A Catholic university may be established by various ecclesiastical authorities or entities (e.g., the Holy See) or by individual Catholics. Moreover, the university may be erected as a self-standing public juridic person or it may be simply be a complex "activity" or "apostolate" of a public juridic person. The following alternatives outline different categories that describe a Catholic university from the canonical perspective:

a) *The university as an apostolate of the Holy See.* The Holy See may erect a university or approve an already-established university as an apostolate of the Holy See itself. Such universities, which are sometimes granted the title of "pontifical," are erected or approved by a decree of the Holy See and their statutes must be approved by the Holy See. The "competent ecclesiastical authority" to which such universities are related is the Holy See through the Congregation for Catholic Education.

b) *The university as an apostolate of the National Conference of Catholic Bishops.* An episcopal conference has the right to erect a university or approve an already-established university as an apostolate of the conference itself through the issuance of a decree and approval of its statutes. The "competent ecclesiastical authority" to which such a university is related is the National Conference of Catholic Bishops.

c) *The university as an apostolate of a diocesan bishop or a group of diocesan bishops.* Diocesan bishops, acting individually or jointly, have the right to erect a university or approve an already-established university as a diocesan or inter-diocesan apostolate through the issuance of a decree and approval of its statutes. The "competent ecclesiastical authority" to which such a university is related is the individual diocesan bishop or the group of diocesan bishops establishing or approving it.

d) *The university as an apostolate of a public juridic person.* A university may be established or approved as an apostolate of a public juridic person (such as a religious institute). In such cases the consent of the bishop of the diocese in which the seat of the university is situated (or of a group of bishops, the NCCB or the Holy See) and approval of its statutes are required. Such a university relates to the public juridic person that established or approved it and to the diocesan bishop (or group of bishops, the NCCB or the Holy See) as its "competent ecclesiastical authority."

e) *The university as public juridic person.* A university may itself be erected as a public association of the faithful or some other type of public juridic person (*universitas rerum or universitas personarum*). Such juridic personality requires the issuance of a decree of erection and approval of the statutes by the Holy See, the National Conference of Catholic Bishops, or an individual or group of diocesan bishops.

f) *The university established by individuals.* Individual Catholics may found a university or convert an existing university into a Catholic institution without its being established or approved by the Holy See, the National Conference of Catholic Bishops, individual diocesan bishops or a public juridic person. Nonetheless, in accordance with canon 808, such a university may refer to itself as Catholic only with the consent of the competent ecclesiastical authority.

[32] *ECE*, II, Art. 3, §4.

[33] C. 808.

[34] *ECE*, II, Art. 4, §1. In these norms the phrases "board of trustees," "president" and "administration" are used to denote the highest bodies of governance within the university's corporate and operational structure. If, in an individual case, the university's governance uses a different structure or other titles, the norms should be applied accordingly.

[35] In individual situations, it may be possible and appropriate to invite the diocesan bishop or his delegate to be a member of the board itself. In other cases, arranging periodic meetings to address the university's Catholic identity and mission may prove more practical and effective.

[36] Upon assuming the office of president for the first time, a Catholic should express his or her commitment to the university's Catholic identity and to the Catholic faith in accordance with canon 833, §7 (*see also* Congregation for the Doctrine of the Faith, Formula *Professio Fidei et Iusiurandum*, July 1, 1988, AAS 81 [1989] 104-106; and Congregation for the Doctrine of the Faith, *Rescriptum ex audientia SS. mi Quod Attinet*, September 19, 1989, AAS 81 [1989] 1169). When a candidate who is not a Catholic is being considered for appointment as president of a Catholic university, the university should consult with the competent ecclesiastical authority about the matter. In all cases, the president should express his or her commitment to the university's Catholic mission and identity.

[37] The identity of a Catholic university is essentially linked to the quality of its professors and to respect for Catholic doctrine. The Church's expectation of "respect for Catholic doctrine" should not, however, be misconstrued to imply that a Catholic university's task is to indoctrinate or proselytize its students. Secular subjects are taught for their intrinsic value, and the teaching of secular subjects is to be measured by the norms and professional standards applicable and appropriate to the individual disciplines. *See ECE*, II, Art. 4, §1 and above footnotes 24 and 27.

[38] C. 810, §1.

[39] *Gravissimum educationis* 10.

[40] C. 812 and *ECE*, II, Art. 4, §3.

[41] "*Mandatum*" is a technical term referring to the juridical expression of the ecclesial relationship of communion that exists between the Church and the Catholic teacher of a theological discipline in the Catholic university. The prescription of canon 812 is grounded in the right and responsibility of bishops to safeguard the faithful teaching of Catholic doctrine to the people of God and to assure the authentic presentation of the Church's magisterium. Those with such a *mandatum* are not agents of the magisterium; they teach in their own name, not in the name of the bishop. Nonetheless, they are not separate from the Church's teaching mission. esponding to their baptismal call, their ecclesial task is to teach, write and research for the benefit of the Church and within its communion. The *mandatum* is essentially the recognition of an ecclesial relationship between the professor and the Church (*see* canon 229, §3).

Moreover, it is not the responsibility of a Catholic university to seek the *mandatum*; this is a personal obligation of each professor. If a particular professor lacks a *mandatum* and continues to teach a theological discipline, the university must determine what further action may be taken in accordance with its own mission and statutes (*see* canon 810, §1).

[42] The attestation or declaration of the professor that he or she will teach in communion with the Church can be expressed by the profession of faith and oath of fidelity or in any other reasonable manner acceptable to the one issuing the *mandatum*.

[43] Although the general principle is that, once granted, there is no need for the *mandatum* to be granted again by another diocesan bishop, every diocesan bishop has the right to require otherwise in his own diocese.

[44] Administrative acts in the external forum must be in writing (c. 37). The writing not only demonstrates the fulfillment of canon 812, but, in cases of denial or removal, it permits the person who considers his or her rights to have been injured to seek recourse. *See* canons 1732-1739.

[45] In *Gravissimum educationis* 10, the Vatican Council expressed the hope that students in Catholic institutions of higher learning will become "truly outstanding in learning, ready to shoulder society's heavier burdens and to witness the faith to the world."

[46] *See* above footnotes 27 and 37.

[47] *See ECE*, I, n. 38 *ff.* and footnote 44.

[48] *See ECE*, I, nn. 48-49.

[49] *See ECE*, II, Art. 5, §2. *See also* the responsibilities of the diocesan bishop set forth in canons 392, §1; 394, §1; 756, §2; 810, §2; 813.

[50] The following are some suggestions for collaboration:

a) Arranging for the diocesan bishop or his delegate and members of the religious institute to be involved in the university's governance, perhaps through representation on the board of trustees or in some other appropriate manner.

b) Sharing the university's annual report with the diocesan bishop and the religious institute, especially in regard to matters affecting Catholic identity and the religious institute's charism.

c) Scheduling regular pastoral visits to the university on the part of the diocesan bishop and the religious institute's leadership and involving the members of the diocese and the institute in campus ministry.

d) Collaborating on evangelization and on the special works of the religious institute.

e) Conducting dialogues on matters of doctrine and pastoral practice and on the development of spirituality in accordance with the religious institute's charism.

f) Resolving issues affecting the university's Catholic identity in accordance with established procedures. (*See ECE*, II, Art. 5, §2 and *ECE* footnote 51.)

g) Participating together in ecumenical and inter-faith endeavors.

h) Contributing to the diocesan process of formulating the quinquennial report to the Holy See.

[51] *See* National Conference of Catholic Bishops, *Doctrinal Responsibilities: Approaches to Promoting Cooperation and Resolving Misunderstandings between Bishops and Theologians*, June 17, 1989, Washington, D.C.: USCC, III, C, pp. 16-22. When such disputes are not resolved within the limits of informal or formal dialogue, they should be addressed in a timely manner by the competent ecclesiastical authority through appropriate doctrinal and administrative actions, taking into account the requirements of the common good and the rights of the individuals and institutions involved.

[52] *See* canon 813

[53] *See ECE*, II, Art. 6, §2.

[54] *See ECE*, II, Art. 7, §1; National Conference of Catholic Bishops, "Sons and Daughters of the Light: A Pastoral Plan for Ministry with Young Adults," *Origins*, November 28, 1996, 384-402, especially 398-401; "Letter to College Students," *Origins*, December 7, 1995, 429-430; *Empowered by the Spirit*, Washington, D.C.: USCC, 1985.

[55] *See ECE*, I, n. 35 and *ECE*, II, Art. 7, §2.

[56] *See ECE*, I, nn. 32-35.

[57] *Ibid.*, Introduction, n. 11.

Instruction on the Ecclesial Vocation of the Theologian

Congregation for the Doctrine of the Faith

Introduction

1. The truth which sets us free is a gift of Jesus Christ (cf. *Jn* 8:32). Man's nature calls him to seek the truth while ignorance keeps him in a condition of servitude. Indeed, man could not be truly free were no light shed upon the central questions of his existence including, in particular, where he comes from and where he is going. When God gives Himself to man as a friend, man becomes free, in accordance with the Lord's word: "No longer do I call you servants, for the servant does not know what his master is doing; but I have called you friends, for all that I have heard from my Father I have made known to you" (*Jn* 15:15). Man's deliverance from the alienation of sin and death comes about when Christ, the Truth, becomes the "way" for him (cf. *Jn* 14:6).

In the Christian faith, knowledge and life, truth and existence are intrinsically connected. Assuredly, the truth given in God's revelation exceeds the capacity of human knowledge, but it is not opposed to human reason. Revelation in fact penetrates human reason, elevates it, and calls it to give an account of itself (cf. *1 Pet* 3:15). For this reason, from the very beginning of the Church, the "standard of teaching" (cf. *Rom* 6:17) has been linked with baptism to entrance into the mystery of Christ. The service of doctrine, implying as it does the believer's search for an understanding of the faith, i.e., theology, is therefore something indispensable for the Church.

Theology has importance for the Church in every age so that it can respond to the plan of God "who desires all men to be saved and to come to

---

Congregation for the Doctrine of the Faith, *Instruction on the Ecclesial Vocation of the Theologian*, May 24, 1990. See http://www.vatican.va/roman_curia/congregations/cfaith/documents/rc_con_cfaith_doc_19900524_theologian-vocation_en.html (accessed October 24, 2005).

the knowledge of the truth" (*1 Tim* 2:4). In times of great spiritual and cultural change, theology is all the more important. Yet it also is exposed to risks since it must strive to "abide" in the truth (cf. *Jn* 8:31), while at the same time taking into account the new problems which confront the human spirit. In our century, in particular, during the periods of preparation for and implementation of the Second Vatican Council, theology contributed much to a deeper "understanding of the realities and the words handed on."[1] But it also experienced and continues to experience moments of crisis and tension.

The Congregation for the Doctrine of the Faith deems it opportune then to address to the Bishops of the Catholic Church, and through them her theologians, the present Instruction which seeks to shed light on the mission of theology in the Church. After having considered truth as God's gift to His people (I), the instruction will describe the role of theologians (II), ponder the particular mission of the Church's Pastors (III), and finally, propose some points on the proper relationship between theologians and pastors (IV). In this way, it aims to serve the growth in understanding of the truth (cf. *Col* 1:10) which ushers us into that freedom which Christ lied and rose to win for us (cf. *Gal* 5:1).

I
The Truth: God's Gift to His People

2. Out of His infinite love, God desired to draw near to man, as he seeks his own proper identity, and walk with him (cf. *Lk* 24:15). He also wanted to free him from the snares of the "father of lies" (cf. *Jn* 8:44) and to open the way to intimacy with Himself so that man could find there, superabundantly, full truth and authentic freedom. This plan of love, conceived by "the Father of lights" (*Jas* 1:17; cf. *1 Pet* 2:9; *1 Jn* 1:5) and realized by the Son victorious over death (cf. *Jn* 8:36), is continually made present by the Spirit who leads "to all truth" (*Jn* 16:13).

3. The truth possesses in itself a unifying force. It frees men from isolation and the oppositions in which they have been trapped by ignorance of the truth. And as it opens the way to God, it, at the same time, unites them to each other. Christ destroyed the wall of separation which had kept them strangers to God's promise and to the fellowship of the covenant (cf. *Eph* 2:12-14). Into the hearts of the faithful He sends His Spirit through whom we become nothing less than "one" in Him (cf. *Rom* 5:5; *Gal* 3:28). Thus thanks to the new birth and the anointing of the Holy Spirit (cf. *Jn* 3:5; *1 Jn* 2:20, 27), we become the one, new People of God whose mission it is, with

our different vocations and charisms, to preserve and hand on the gift of truth. Indeed, the whole Church, as the "salt of the earth" and "the light of the world" (cf. *Mt* 5:13 f.), must bear witness to the truth of Christ which sets us free.

4. The People of God respond to this calling "above all by means of the life of faith and charity, and by offering to God a sacrifice of praise." More specifically, as far as the "life of faith" is concerned, the Second Vatican Council makes it clear that "the whole body of the faithful who have an anointing that comes from the holy one (cf. *1 Jn* 2:20, 27) cannot err in matters of belief." And "this characteristic is shown in the supernatural sense of the faith of the whole people, when 'from the bishops to the last of the faithful' they manifest a universal consent in matters of faith and morals."[2]

5. In order to exercise the prophetic function in the world, the People of God must continually reawaken or "rekindle" its own life of faith (cf. *2 Tim* 1:6). It does this particularly by contemplating ever more deeply, under the guidance of the Holy Spirit, the contents of the faith itself and by dutifully presenting the reasonableness of the faith to those who ask for an account of it (cf. *1 Pet* 3:15). For the sake of this mission, the Spirit of truth distributes among the faithful of every rank special graces "for the common good" (*1 Cor* 12:7-11).

II
The Vocation of the Theologian

6. Among the vocations awakened in this way by the Spirit in the Church is that of the theologian. His role is to pursue in a particular way an ever deeper understanding of the Word of God found in the inspired Scriptures and handed on by the living Tradition of the Church. He does this in communion with the Magisterium, which has been charged with the responsibility of preserving the deposit of faith.

By its nature, faith appeals to reason because it reveals to man the truth of his destiny and the way to attain it. Revealed truth, to be sure, surpasses our telling. All our concepts fall short of its ultimately unfathomable grandeur (cf. *Eph* 3:19). Nonetheless, revealed truth beckons reason—God's gift fashioned for the assimilation of truth—to enter into its light and thereby come to understand in a certain measure what it has believed. Theological science responds to the invitation of truth as it seeks to understand the faith. It thereby aids the People of God in fulfilling the Apostle's command (cf. *1 Pet* 3:15) to give an accounting for their hope to those who ask it.

7. The theologian's work thus responds to a dynamism found in the faith itself. Truth, by its nature, seeks to be communicated since man was created for the perception of truth and from the depths of his being desires knowledge of it so that he can discover himself in the truth and find there his salvation (cf. *1 Tim* 2:4). For this reason, the Lord sent forth His apostles to make "disciples" of all nations and teach them (cf. *Mt* 28:19 f.). Theology, which seeks the "reasons of faith" and offers these reasons as a response to those seeking them, thus constitutes an integral part of obedience to the command of Christ, for men cannot become disciples if the truth found in the word of faith is not presented to them (cf. *Rom* 10:14 f.).

Theology therefore offers its contribution so that the faith might be communicated. Appealing to the understanding of those who do not yet know Christ, it helps them to seek and find faith. Obedient to the impulse of truth which seeks to be communicated, theology also arises from love and love's dynamism. In the act of faith, man knows God's goodness and begins to love Him. Love, however, is ever desirous of a better knowledge of the beloved.[3] From this double origin of theology, inscribed upon the interior life of the People of God and its missionary vocation, derives the method with which it ought to be pursued in order to satisfy the requirements of its nature.

8. Since the object of theology is the Truth which is the living God and His plan for salvation revealed in Jesus Christ, the theologian is called to deepen his own life of faith and continuously unite his scientific research with prayer.[4] In this way, he will become more open to the "supernatural sense of faith" upon which he depends, and it will appear to him as a sure rule for guiding his reflections and helping him assess the correctness of his conclusions.

9. Through the course of centuries, theology has progressively developed into a true and proper science. The theologian must therefore be attentive to the epistemological requirements of his discipline, to the demands of rigorous critical standards, and thus to a rational verification of each stage of his research. The obligation to be critical, however, should not be identified with the critical spirit which is born of feeling or prejudice. The theologian must discern in himself the origin of and motivation for his critical attitude and allow his gaze to be purified by faith. The commitment to theology requires a spiritual effort to grow in virtue and holiness.

10. Even though it transcends human reason, revealed truth is in profound harmony with it. It presumes that reason by its nature is ordered to the truth in such a way that, illumined by faith, it can penetrate to the meaning of Revelation. Despite the assertions of many philosophical currents, but in conformity with a correct way of thinking which finds confirmation in Scrip-

ture, human reason's ability to attain truth must be recognized as well as its metaphysical capacity to come to a knowledge of God from creation.[5]

Theology's proper task is to understand the meaning of revelation and this, therefore, requires the utilization of philosophical concepts which provide "a solid and correct understanding of man, the world, and God"[6] and can be employed in a reflection upon revealed doctrine. The historical disciplines are likewise necessary for the theologian's investigations. This is due chiefly to the historical character of revelation itself which has been communicated to us in "salvation history." Finally, a consultation of the "human sciences" is also necessary to understand better the revealed truth about man and the moral norms for his conduct, setting these in relation to the sound findings of such sciences.

It is the theologian's task in this perspective to draw from the surrounding culture those elements which will allow him better to illumine one or other aspect of the mysteries of faith. This is certainly an arduous task that has its risks, but it is legitimate in itself and should be encouraged.

Here it is important to emphasize that when theology employs the elements and conceptual tools of philosophy or other disciplines, discernment is needed. The ultimate normative principle for such discernment is revealed doctrine which itself must furnish the criteria for the evaluation of these elements and conceptual tools and not *vice versa*.

11. Never forgetting that he is also a member of the People of God, the theologian must foster respect for them and be committed to offering them a teaching which in no way does harm to the doctrine of the faith.

The freedom proper to theological research is exercised within the Church's faith. Thus while the theologian might often feel the urge to be daring in his work, this will not bear fruit or "edify" unless it is accompanied by that patience which permits maturation to occur. New proposals advanced for understanding the faith "are but an offering made to the whole Church. Many corrections and broadening of perspectives within the context of fraternal dialogue may be needed before the moment comes when the whole Church can accept them." Consequently, "this very disinterested service to the community of the faithful," which theology is, "entails in essence an objective discussion, a fraternal dialogue, an openness and willingness to modify one's own opinions."[7]

12. Freedom of research, which the academic community rightly holds most precious, means an openness to accepting the truth that emerges at the end of an investigation in which no element has intruded that is foreign to the methodology corresponding to the object under study.

In theology this freedom of inquiry is the hallmark of a rational discipline whose object is given by Revelation, handed on and interpreted in the Church under the authority of the Magisterium, and received by faith. These givens have the force of principles. To eliminate them would mean to cease doing theology. In order to set forth precisely the ways in which the theologian relates to the Church's teaching authority, it is appropriate now to reflect upon the role of the Magisterium in the Church.

II
The Magisterium of the Church's Pastors

13. "God graciously arranged that the things he had once revealed for the salvation of all peoples should remain in their entirety, throughout the ages, and be transmitted to all generations."[8] He bestowed upon His Church, through the gift of the Holy Spirit, a participation in His own infallibility.[9] Thanks to the "supernatural sense of Faith," the People of God enjoys this privilege under the guidance of the Church's living Magisterium, which is the sole authentic interpreter of the Word of God, written or handed down, by virtue of the authority which it exercises in the name of Christ.[10]

14. As successors of the apostles, the bishops of the Church "receive from the Lord, to whom all power is given in heaven and on earth, the mission of teaching all peoples, and of preaching the Gospel to every creature, so that all men may attain to salvation. . . ."[11] They have been entrusted then with the task of preserving, explaining, and spreading the Word of God of which they are servants.[12]

It is the mission of the Magisterium to affirm the definitive character of the Covenant established by God through Christ with His People in a way which is consistent with the "eschatological" nature of the event of Jesus Christ. It must protect God's People from the danger of deviations and confusion, guaranteeing them the objective possibility of professing the authentic faith free from error, at all times and in diverse situations. It follows that the sense and the weight of the Magisterium's authority are only intelligible in relation to the truth of Christian doctrine and the preaching of the true Word. The function of the Magisterium is not, then, something extrinsic to Christian truth nor is it set above the faith. It arises directly from the economy of the faith itself, inasmuch as the Magisterium is, in its service to the Word of God, an institution positively willed by Christ as a constitutive element of His Church. The service to Christian truth which the Magisterium renders is thus for the benefit of the whole People of God called to enter the liberty of the truth revealed by God in Christ.

15. Jesus Christ promised the assistance of the Holy Spirit to the Church's Pastors so that they could fulfill their assigned task of teaching the Gospel and authentically interpreting Revelation. In particular, He bestowed on them the charism of infallibility in matters of faith and morals. This charism is manifested when the Pastors propose a doctrine as contained in Revelation and can be exercised in various ways. Thus it is exercised particularly when the bishops in union with their visible head proclaim a doctrine by a collegial act, as is the case in an ecumenical council, or when the Roman Pontiff, fulfilling his mission as supreme Pastor and Teacher of all Christians, proclaims a doctrine *"ex cathedra."* [13]

16. By its nature, the task of religiously guarding and loyally expounding the deposit of divine Revelation (in all its integrity and purity), implies that the Magisterium can make a pronouncement "in a definitive way" [14] on propositions which, even if not contained among the truths of faith, are nonetheless intimately connected with them, in such a way, that the definitive character of such affirmations derives in the final analysis from revelation itself. [15]

What concerns morality can also be the object of the authentic Magisterium because the Gospel, being the Word of Life, inspires and guides the whole sphere of human behavior. The Magisterium, therefore, has the task of discerning, by means of judgments normative for the consciences of believers, those acts which in themselves conform to the demands of faith and foster their expression in life and those which, on the contrary, because intrinsically evil, are incompatible with such demands. By reason of the connection between the orders of creation and redemption and by reason of the necessity, in view of salvation, of knowing and observing the whole moral law, the competence of the Magisterium also extends to that which concerns the natural law. [16]

Revelation also contains moral teachings which *per se* could be known by natural reason. Access to them, however, is made difficult by man's sinful condition. It is a doctrine of faith that these moral norms can be infallibly taught by the Magisterium. [17]

17. Divine assistance is also given to the successors of the apostles teaching in communion with the successor of Peter, and in a particular way, to the Roman Pontiff as Pastor of the whole Church, when exercising their ordinary Magisterium, even should this not issue in an infallible definition or in a "definitive" pronouncement but in the proposal of some teaching which leads to a better understanding of Revelation in matters of faith and morals and to moral directives derived from such teaching.

One must therefore take into account the proper character of every exercise of the Magisterium, considering the extent to which its authority is engaged. It is also to be borne in mind that all acts of the Magisterium derive from the same source, that is, from Christ who desires that His People walk in the entire truth. For this same reason, magisterial decisions in matters of discipline, even if they are not guaranteed by the charism of infallibility, are not without divine assistance and call for the adherence of the faithful.

18. The Roman Pontiff fulfills his universal mission with the help of the various bodies of the Roman Curia and in particular with that of the Congregation for the Doctrine of the Faith in matters of doctrine and morals. Consequently, the documents issued by this Congregation expressly approved by the Pope participate in the ordinary magisterium of the successor of Peter.[18]

19. Within the particular Churches, it is the bishop's responsibility to guard and interpret the Word of God and to make authoritative judgments as to what is or is not in conformity with it. The teaching of each bishop, taken individually, is exercised in communion with the Roman Pontiff, Pastor of the universal Church, and with the other bishops dispersed throughout the world or gathered in an ecumenical council. Such communion is a condition for its authenticity.

Member of the Episcopal College by virtue of his sacramental ordination and hierarchical communion, the bishop represents his Church just as all the bishops, in union with the Pope, represent the Church universal in the bonds of peace, love, unity, and truth. As they come together in unity, the local Churches, with their own proper patrimonies, manifest the Church's catholicity. The episcopal conferences for their part contribute to the concrete realization of the collegial spirit (*"affectus"*).[19]

20. The pastoral task of the Magisterium is one of vigilance. It seeks to ensure that the People of God remain in the truth which sets free. It is therefore a complex and diversified reality. The theologian, to be faithful to his role of service to the truth, must take into account the proper mission of the Magisterium and collaborate with it. How should this collaboration be understood? How is it put into practice and what are the obstacles it may face? These questions should now be examined more closely.

IV
The Magisterium and Theology

A. Collaborative Relations

21. The living Magisterium of the Church and theology, while having different gifts and functions, ultimately have the same goal: preserving the People of God in the truth which sets free and thereby making them "a light

to the nations." This service to the ecclesial community brings the theologian and the Magisterium into a reciprocal relationship. The latter authentically teaches the doctrine of the Apostles. And, benefiting from the work of theologians, it refutes objections to and distortions of the faith and promotes, with the authority received from Jesus Christ, new and deeper comprehension, clarification, and application of revealed doctrine. Theology, for its part, gains, by way of reflection, an ever deeper understanding of the Word of God found in the Scripture and handed on faithfully by the Church's living Tradition under the guidance of the Magisterium. Theology strives to clarify the teaching of Revelation with regard to reason and gives it finally an organic and systematic form.[20]

22. Collaboration between the theologian and the Magisterium occurs in a special way when the theologian receives the canonical mission or the mandate to teach. In a certain sense, such collaboration becomes a participation in the work of the Magisterium, linked, as it then is, by a juridic bond. The theologian's code of conduct, which obviously has its origin in the service of the Word of God, is here reinforced by the commitment the theologian assumes in accepting his office, making the profession of faith, and taking the oath of fidelity.[21]

From this moment on, the theologian is officially charged with the task of presenting and illustrating the doctrine of the faith in its integrity and with full accuracy.

23. When the Magisterium of the Church makes an infallible pronouncement and solemnly declares that a teaching is found in Revelation, the assent called for is that of theological faith. This kind of adherence is to be given even to the teaching of the ordinary and universal Magisterium when it proposes for belief a teaching of faith as divinely revealed.

When the Magisterium proposes "in a definitive way" truths concerning faith and morals, which, even if not divinely revealed, are nevertheless strictly and intimately connected with Revelation, these must be firmly accepted and held.[22]

When the Magisterium, not intending to act "definitively," teaches a doctrine to aid a better understanding of Revelation and make explicit its contents, or to recall how some teaching is in conformity with the truths of faith, or finally to guard against ideas that are incompatible with these truths, the response called for is that of the religious submission of will and intellect.[23] This kind of response cannot be simply exterior or disciplinary but must be understood within the logic of faith and under the impulse of obedience to the faith.

24. Finally, in order to serve the People of God as well as possible, in particular, by warning them of dangerous opinions which could lead to error, the Magisterium can intervene in questions under discussion which involve, in addition to solid principles, certain contingent and conjectural elements. It often only becomes possible with the passage of time to distinguish between what is necessary and what is contingent.

The willingness to submit loyally to the teaching of the Magisterium on matters *per se* not irreformable must be the rule. It can happen, however, that a theologian may, according to the case, raise questions regarding the timeliness, the form, or even the contents of magisterial interventions. Here the theologian will need, first of all, to assess accurately the authoritativeness of the interventions which becomes clear from the nature of the documents, the insistence with which a teaching is repeated, and the very way in which it is expressed.[24]

When it comes to the question of interventions in the prudential order, it could happen that some Magisterial documents might not be free from all deficiencies. Bishops and their advisors have not always taken into immediate consideration every aspect or the entire complexity of a question. But it would be contrary to the truth, if, proceeding from some particular cases, one were to conclude that the Church's Magisterium can be habitually mistaken in its prudential judgments, or that it does not enjoy divine assistance in the integral exercise of its mission. In fact, the theologian, who cannot pursue his discipline well without a certain competence in history, is aware of the filtering which occurs with the passage of time. This is not to be understood in the sense of a relativization of the tenets of the faith. The theologian knows that some judgments of the Magisterium could be justified at the time in which they were made, because while the pronouncements contained true assertions and others which were not sure, both types were inextricably connected. Only time has permitted discernment and, after deeper study, the attainment of true doctrinal progress.

25. Even when collaboration takes place under the best conditions, the possibility cannot be excluded that tensions may arise between the theologian and the Magisterium. The meaning attributed to such tensions and the spirit with which they are faced are not matters of indifference. If tensions do not spring from hostile and contrary feelings, they can become a dynamic factor, a stimulus to both the Magisterium and theologians to fulfill their respective roles while practicing dialogue.

26. In the dialogue, a two-fold rule should prevail. When there is a question of the communion of faith, the principle of the "unity of truth" (*unitas ver-*

itatis) applies. When it is a question of differences which do not jeopardize this communion, the "unity of charity" (*unitas caritatis*) should be safeguarded.

27. Even if the doctrine of the faith is not in question, the theologian will not present his own opinions or divergent hypotheses as though they were non-arguable conclusions. Respect for the truth as well as for the People of God requires this discretion (cf. *Rom* 14:1-15; *1 Cor* 8; 10: 23-33). For the same reasons, the theologian will refrain from giving untimely public expression to them.

28. The preceding considerations have a particular application to the case of the theologian who might have serious difficulties, for reasons which appear to him well founded, in accepting a non-irreformable magisterial teaching.

Such a disagreement could not be justified if it were based solely upon the fact that the validity of the given teaching is not evident or upon the opinion that the opposite position would be the more probable. Nor, furthermore, would the judgment of the subjective conscience of the theologian justify it because conscience does not constitute an autonomous and exclusive authority for deciding the truth of a doctrine.

29. In any case there should never be a diminishment of that fundamental openness loyally to accept the teaching of the Magisterium, as is fitting for every believer by reason of the obedience of faith. The theologian will strive then to understand this teaching in its contents, arguments, and purposes. This will mean an intense and patient reflection on his part and a readiness, if need be, to revise his own opinions and examine the objections which his colleagues might offer him.

30. If, despite a loyal effort on the theologian's part, the difficulties persist, the theologian has the duty to make known to the Magisterial authorities the problems raised by the teaching in itself, in the arguments proposed to justify it, or even in the manner in which it is presented. He should do this in an evangelical spirit and with a profound desire to resolve the difficulties. His objections could then contribute to real progress and provide a stimulus to the Magisterium to propose the teaching of the Church in greater depth and with a clearer presentation of the arguments.

In cases like these, the theologian should avoid turning to the "mass media," but have recourse to the responsible authority, for it is not by seeking to exert the pressure of public opinion that one contributes to the clarification of doctrinal issues and renders service to the truth.

31. It can also happen that at the conclusion of a serious study, undertaken with the desire to heed the Magisterium's teaching without hesitation, the theologian's difficulty remains because the arguments to the contrary seem more persuasive to him. Faced with a proposition to which he feels he

cannot give his intellectual assent, the theologian nevertheless has the duty to remain open to a deeper examination of the question.

For a loyal spirit, animated by love for the Church, such a situation can certainly prove a difficult trial. It can be a call to suffer for the truth, in silence and prayer, but with the certainty that if the truth really is at stake, it will ultimately prevail.

A. The Problem of Dissent

32. The Magisterium has drawn attention several times to the serious harm done to the community of the Church by attitudes of general opposition to Church teaching which even come to expression in organized groups. In his apostolic exhortation *Paterna cum benevolentia*, Paul VI offered a diagnosis of this problem which is still apropos.[25] In particular, he addresses here that public opposition to the Magisterium of the Church is also called "dissent," which must be distinguished from the situation of personal difficulties treated above. The phenomenon of dissent can have diverse forms. Its remote and proximate causes are multiple.

The ideology of philosophical liberalism, which permeates the thinking of our age, must be counted among the factors which may exercise their remote or indirect influence. Here arises the tendency to regard a judgment as having all the more validity to the extent that it proceeds from the individual relying upon his own powers. In such a way freedom of thought comes to oppose the authority of tradition which is considered a cause of servitude. A teaching handed on and generally received is *a priori* suspect and its truth contested. Ultimately, freedom of judgment understood in this way is more important than the truth itself. We are dealing then here with something quite different from the legitimate demand for freedom in the sense of absence of constraint as a necessary condition for the loyal inquiry into truth. In virtue of this exigency, the Church has always held that "nobody is to be forced to embrace the faith against his will."[26]

The weight of public opinion when manipulated and its pressure to conform also have their influence. Often models of society promoted by the "mass media" tend to assume a normative value. The view is particularly promoted that the Church should only express her judgment on those issues which public opinion considers important and then only by way of agreeing with it. The Magisterium, for example, could intervene in economic or social questions but ought to leave matters of conjugal and family morality to individual judgment.

Finally, the plurality of cultures and languages, in itself a benefit, can indirectly bring on misunderstandings which occasion disagreements.

In this context, the theologian needs to make a critical, well-considered discernment, as well as have a true mastery of the issues, if he wants to fulfill his ecclesial mission and not lose, by conforming himself to this present world (cf. *Rom* 12:2; *Eph* 4:23), the independence of judgment which should be that of the disciples of Christ.

33. Dissent has different aspects. In its most radical form, it aims at changing the Church following a model of protest which takes its inspiration from political society. More frequently, it is asserted that the theologian is not bound to adhere to any Magisterial teaching unless it is infallible. Thus a kind of theological positivism is adopted, according to which, doctrines proposed without exercise of the charism of infallibility are said to have no obligatory character about them, leaving the individual completely at liberty to adhere to them or not. The theologian would accordingly be totally free to raise doubts or reject the non-infallible teaching of the Magisterium particularly in the case of specific moral norms. With such critical opposition, he would even be making a contribution to the development of doctrine.

34. Dissent is generally defended by various arguments, two of which are more basic in character. The first lies in the order of hermeneutics. The documents of the Magisterium, it is said, reflect nothing more than a debatable theology. The second takes theological pluralism sometimes to the point of a relativism which calls the integrity of the faith into question. Here the interventions of the Magisterium would have their origin in one theology among many theologies, while no particular theology, however, could presume to claim universal normative status. In opposition to and in competition with the authentic Magisterium, there thus arises a kind of "parallel magisterium" of theologians.[27]

Certainly, it is one of the theologian's tasks to give a correct interpretation to the texts of the Magisterium and to this end he employs various hermeneutical rules. Among these is the principle which affirms that Magisterial teaching, by virtue of divine assistance, has a validity beyond its argumentation, which may derive at times from a particular theology. As far as theological pluralism is concerned, this is only legitimate to the extent that the unity of the faith in its objective meaning is not jeopardized.[28] Essential bonds link the distinct levels of unity of faith, unity-plurality of expressions of the faith, and plurality of theologies. The ultimate reason for plurality is found in the unfathomable mystery of Christ who transcends every objective systematization. This cannot mean that it is possible to accept conclusions contrary to that mystery and it certainly does not put into question the truth of those assertions by which the Magisterium has declared itself.[29] As to the "parallel magisterium," it can cause great spiritual harm by opposing itself to the Magisterium of the Pastors. Indeed, when dissent succeeds in extending its influence to the point of shaping a common opinion, it tends to become the rule of conduct. This cannot but seriously trouble the People of God and lead to contempt for true authority.[30]

35. Dissent sometimes also appeals to a kind of sociological argumentation which holds that the opinion of a large number of Christians would be a direct and adequate expression of the "supernatural sense of the faith."

Actually, the opinions of the faithful cannot be purely and simply identified with the "*sensus fidei.*"[31] The sense of the faith is a property of theological faith; and, as God's gift which enables one to adhere personally to the Truth, it cannot err. This personal faith is also the faith of the Church since God has given guardianship of the Word to the Church. Consequently, what the believer believes is what the Church believes. The "*sensus fidei*" implies then by its nature a profound agreement of spirit and heart with the Church, "*sentire cum Ecclesia.*"

Although theological faith as such then cannot err, the believer can still have erroneous opinions since all his thoughts do not spring from faith.[32] Not all the ideas which circulate among the People of God are compatible with the faith. This is all the more so given that people can be swayed by a public opinion influenced by modern communications media. Not without reason did the Second Vatican Council emphasize the indissoluble bond between the "*sensus fidei*" and the guidance of God's People by the Magisterium of the Pastors. These two realities cannot be separated.[33] Magisterial interventions serve to guarantee the Church's unity in the truth of the Lord. They aid her to "abide in the truth" in face of the arbitrary character of changeable opinions and are an expression of obedience to the Word of God.[34] Even when it might seem that they limit the freedom of theologians, these actions, by their fidelity to the faith which has been handed on, establish a deeper freedom which can only come from unity in truth.

36. The freedom of the act of faith cannot justify a right to dissent. In fact this freedom does not indicate at all freedom with regard to the truth but signifies the free self-determination of the person in conformity with his moral obligation to accept the truth. The act of faith is a voluntary act because man, saved by Christ the Redeemer and called by Him to be an adopted son (cf. *Rom* 8:15; *Gal* 4:5; *Eph* 1:5; *Jn* 1:12), cannot adhere to God unless, "drawn by the Father" (*Jn* 6:44), he offer God the rational homage of

his faith (cf. *Rom* 12:1). As the Declaration *Dignitatis humanae* recalls,[35] no human authority may overstep the limits of its competence and claim the right to interfere with this choice by exerting pressure or constraint. Respect for religious liberty is the foundation of respect for all the rights of man.

One cannot then appeal to these rights of man in order to oppose the interventions of the Magisterium. Such behavior fails to recognize the nature and mission of the Church which has received from the Lord the task to proclaim the truth of salvation to all men. She fulfills this task by walking in Christ's footsteps, knowing that "truth can impose itself on the mind only by virtue of its own truth, which wins over the mind with both gentleness and power."[36]

37. By virtue of the divine mandate given to it in the Church, the Magisterium has the mission to set forth the Gospel's teaching, guard its integrity, and thereby protect the Faith of the People of God. In order to fulfill this duty, it can at times be led to take serious measures as, for example, when it withdraws from a theologian, who departs from the doctrine of the faith, the canonical mission or the teaching mandate it had given him, or declares that some writings do not conform to this doctrine. When it acts in such ways, the Magisterium seeks to be faithful to its mission of defending the right of the People of God to receive the message of the Church in its purity and integrity and not be disturbed by a particular dangerous opinion.

The judgment expressed by the Magisterium in such circumstances is the result of a thorough investigation conducted according to established procedures which afford the interested party the opportunity to clear up possible misunderstandings of his thought. This judgment, however, does not concern the person of the theologian but the intellectual positions which he has publicly espoused. The fact that these procedures can be improved does not mean that they are contrary to justice and right. To speak in this instance of a violation of human rights is out of place for it indicates a failure to recognize the proper hierarchy of these rights as well as the nature of the ecclesial community and her common good. Moreover, the theologian who is not disposed to think with the Church ("*sentire cum Ecclesia*") contradicts the commitment he freely and knowingly accepted to teach in the name of the Church.[37]

38. Finally, argumentation appealing to the obligation to follow one's own conscience cannot legitimate dissent. This is true, first of all, because conscience illumines the practical judgment about a decision to make, while here we are concerned with the truth of a doctrinal pronouncement. This is furthermore the case because while the theologian, like every believer, must follow his conscience, he is also obliged to form it. Conscience is not an

independent and infallible faculty. It is an act of moral judgment regarding a responsible choice. A right conscience is one duly illumined by faith and by the objective moral law and it presupposes, as well, the uprightness of the will in the pursuit of the true good.

The right conscience of the Catholic theologian presumes not only faith in the Word of God whose riches he must explore, but also love for the Church from whom he receives his mission, and respect for her divinely assisted Magisterium. Setting up a supreme magisterium of conscience in opposition to the Magisterium of the Church means adopting a principle of free examination incompatible with the economy of Revelation and its transmission in the Church and thus also with a correct understanding of theology and the role of the theologian. The propositions of faith are not the product of mere individual research and free criticism of the Word of God but constitute an ecclesial heritage. If there occur a separation from the Bishops who watch over and keep the apostolic tradition alive, it is the bond with Christ which is irreparably compromised.[38]

39. The Church, which has her origin in the unity of the Father, Son, and Holy Spirit,[39] is a mystery of communion. In accordance with the will of her founder, she is organized around a hierarchy established for the service of the Gospel and the People of God who live by it. After the pattern of the members of the first community, all the baptized with their own proper charisms are to strive with sincere hearts for a harmonious unity in doctrine, life, and worship (cf. *Acts* 2:42). This is a rule which flows from the very being of the Church. For this reason, standards of conduct, appropriate to civil society or the workings of a democracy, cannot be purely and simply applied to the Church. Even less can relationships within the Church be inspired by the mentality of the world around it (cf. *Rom* 12:2). Polling public opinion to determine the proper thing to think or do, opposing the Magisterium by exerting the pressure of public opinion, making the excuse of a "consensus" among theologians, maintaining that the theologian is the prophetical spokesman of a "base" or autonomous community which would be the source of all truth, all this indicates a grave loss of the sense of truth and of the sense of the Church.

40. The Church "is like a sacrament, a sign and instrument, that is, of communion with God and of unity among all men."[40] Consequently, to pursue concord and communion is to enhance the force of her witness and credibility. To succumb to the temptation of dissent, on the other hand, is to allow the "leaven of infidelity to the Holy Spirit" to start to work.[41]

To be sure, theology and the Magisterium are of diverse natures and missions and cannot be confused. Nonetheless they fulfill two vital roles in the Church which must interpenetrate and enrich each other for the service of the People of God.

It is the duty of the Pastors by virtue of the authority they have received from Christ Himself to guard this unity and to see that the tensions arising from life do not degenerate into divisions. Their authority, which transcends particular positions and oppositions, must unite all in the integrity of the Gospel which is the "word of reconciliation" (cf. *2 Cor* 5:18-20).

As for theologians, by virtue of their own proper charisms, they have the responsibility of participating in the building up of Christ's Body in unity and truth. Their contribution is needed more than ever, for evangelization on a world scale requires the efforts of the whole People of God.[42] If it happens that they encounter difficulties due to the character of their research, they should seek their solution in trustful dialogue with the Pastors, in the spirit of truth and charity which is that of the communion of the Church.

41. Both Bishops and theologians will keep in mind that Christ is the definitive Word of the Father (cf. *Heb* 1:2) in whom, as St. John of the Cross observes: "God has told us everything all together and at one time."[43] As such, He is the Truth who sets us free (cf. *Jn* 8:36; 14:6). The acts of assent and submission to the Word entrusted to the Church under the guidance of the Magisterium are directed ultimately to Him and lead us into the realm of true freedom.

Conclusion

42. The Virgin Mary is Mother and perfect Icon of the Church. From the very beginnings of the New Testament, she has been called blessed because of her immediate and unhesitating assent of faith to the Word of God (cf. *Lk* 1:38, 45) which she kept and pondered in her heart (cf. *Lk* 2:19, 51). Thus did she become a model and source of help for all of the People of God entrusted to her maternal care. She shows us the way to accept and serve the Word. At the same time, she points out the final goal, on which our sights should ever be set, the salvation won for the world by her Son Jesus Christ which we are to proclaim to all men.

At the close of this Instruction, the Congregation for the Doctrine of the Faith earnestly invites Bishops to maintain and develop relations of trust with theologians in the fellowship of charity and in the realization that they share one spirit in their acceptance and service of the Word. In this context, they will more easily overcome some of the obstacles which are part of the human condition on earth. In this way, all can become ever better servants of the Word and of the People of God, so that the People of God, persevering in the doctrine of truth and freedom heard from the beginning, may abide also in the Son and the Father and obtain eternal life, the fulfillment of the Promise (cf. 1 Jn 2:24-25).

This Instruction was adopted at a Plenary Meeting of the Congregation for the Doctrine of the Faith and was approved at an audience granted to the undersigned Cardinal Prefect by the Supreme Pontiff, Pope John Paul II, who ordered its publication.

Given at Rome, at the Congregation for the Doctrine of the Faith, on May 24, 1990, the Solemnity of the Ascension of the Lord.

JOSEPH CARD. RATZINGER
Prefect

✠ ALBERTO BOVONE
Titular Archbishop of Caesaria in Numidia
Secretary

NOTES

[1] Dogmatic Constitution *Dei Verbum*, n. 8.

[2] Dogmatic Constitution *Lumen gentium*, n. 12.

[3] Cf. St. Bonaventure, *Prooem. in I Sent.*, q. 2, ad 6: "Quando fides non assentit propter rationem, sed propter amorem eius cui assentit, desiderat habere rationes."

[4] Cf. John Paul II, "Discorso in occasione della consegna del premio internazionale Paulo VI a Hans Urs von Balthasar," June 23, 1984: Insegnamenti di Giovanni Paolo II. VII, 1 (1984) 1911-1917.

[5] Cf. Vatican Council. I, Dogmatic Constitution *De fide catholica, De revelatione*, can. l: DS 3026.

[6] Decree *Optatam totius*, n. 15.

[7] John Paul II, "Discorso ai teologi ad Altötting," November 18, 1980: AAS 73 (1981) 104; cf. also Paul VI, "Discorso ai membri della Commissione Teologica Internazionale," October 11, 1972: AAS 64 (1972) 682-683; John Paul II, "Discorso ai membri della Commissione Teologica Internazionale," October 26, 1979: AAS 71 (1979) 1428-1433.

[8] Dogmatic Constitution *Dei Verbum*, n. 7.

[9] Cf. Congregation for the Doctrine of the Faith, Decl. *Mysterium Ecclesiae*. n. 2:AAS 65 (1973) 398 f.

[10] Cf. Dogmatic Constitution *Dei Verbum*, n. 10.

[11] Dogmatic Constitution *Lumen gentium*, n. 24.

[12] Cf. Dogmatic Constitution *Dei Verbum*, n. 10.

[13] Cf. Dogmatic Constitution *Lumen gentium*, n. 25; Congregation for the Doctrine of the Faith, Decl. *Mysterium Ecclesiae*, n. 3: AAS 65 (1973) 400 f.

[14] Cf. *Professio fidei et Iusiurrandum fidelitatis*: AAS 81 (1989) 104 f.: "omnia et singula quae circa doctrinam de fide vel moribus ab eadem definitive proponuntur."

[15] Cf. Dogmatic Constitution *Lumen gentium*, n. 25; Congregation for the Doctrine of the Faith, Decl. Mysterium Ecclesiae, nn. 3-5: AAS 65 (1973) 400-404; *Professio fidei et Iusiurandum fidelitatis* AAS 81 (1989) 104 f.

[16] Cf. Paul VI, Encycl. *Humanae Vitae*, n. 4: AAS 60 (1968), 483.

[17] Cf. Vatican Council, I, Dogmatic Constitution *Dei Filius*, ch. 2: DS 3005.

[18] Cf. *Code of Canon Law*, cc. 360-361; Paul VI, Apost. Const. *Regimini Ecclesiae Universae*, August 15, 1967, nn. 29-40: AAS 59 (1967) 879-899; John Paul II, Apost. Const. *Pastor Bonus*, June 28, 1988: AAS 80 (1988) 873-874.

[19] Dogmatic Constitution *Lumen Gentium*, nn. 22-23. As it is known, following upon the Second Extraordinary Synod of Bishops, the Holy Father gave the Congregation for Bishops the task of exploring the "Theological-Juridical Status of Episcopal Conferences."

[20] Cf. Paul VI, "Discorso ai partecipanti al Congresso internazionale suila Teologia del Concilio Vaticano II," October 1, 1966: *Insegnamenti di Paolo VI*: AAS 58 (1966) 892 f.

[21] Cf. *Code of Canon Law*, can. 833; *Professio fidei et Iusiurandum fidelitatis*: AAS 81 (1989) 104 ff.

[22] The text of the new Profession of Faith (cf. n. 15) makes explicit the kind of assent called for by these teachings in these terms: "Firmiter etiam amplector et retineo. . . ."

[23] Cf. Dogmatic Constitution *Lumen Gentium*, n. 25; *Code of Canon Law*, can. 752.

[24] Dogmatic Constitution *Lumen Gentium*, n. 25, § 1.

[25] Cf. Paul VI, Apost. Exhort. *Paterna cum benevolentia*, December 8, 1974: AAS 67 (1975) 5-23. Cf. also Congregation for the Doctrine of the Faith, Decl. *Mysterium Ecclesiae*: AAS 65 (1973) 396-408.

[26] Decl. *Dignitatis humanae*, n. 10.

[27] The notion of a "parallel magisterium" of theologians in opposition to and in competition with the Magisterium of the Pastors is sometimes supported by reference to some texts in which St. Thomas Aquinas makes a distinction between the "magisterium cathedrae pastoralis" and "magisterium cathedrae magisterialis" (*Contro impugnantes*, c. 2; *Quodlib.* III, q. 4, a.l (9); *In IV.Sent.* 19, 2, 2, q.3 sol. 2 ad 4). Actually, these texts do not give any support to this position for St. Thomas was absolutely certain that the right to judge in matters of doctrine was the sole responsibility of the "officium praelationis."

[28] Paul VI, Apost. Export. *Paterna cum benevolentia*, n. 4: AAS 67 (1975) 14-15.

[29] Cf. Paul VI, "Discorso ai membri della Commissione Teologica Internazionale," October 11, 1973: AAS 65 (1973) 555-559.

[30] Cf. John Paul II, Encyc. *Redemptor hominis*, n. 19: AAS 71 (1979) 308; "Discorso ai fedeli di Managua," March 4, 1983, n. 7: AAS 75 (1983) 723; "Discorso ai religiosi a Guatemala," March 8, 1983, n. 3: AAS 75 (1983) 746; "Discorso ai vescovi a Lima," February 2, 1985, n. 5: AAS 77 (1985) 874; "Discorso alla Conferenza dei vescovi belgi a Malines," May 18, 1985, n. 5: Insegnamenti di Giovanni Paolo II, VIII, 1 (1985) 1481; "Discorso ad alcuni vescovi americani in visita ad limina," October 15, 1988, n. 6: L'Osservatore Romano, October 16, 1988. p. 4.

[31] Cf. John Paul. II, Apost. Exhort. *Familiaris consortio*, n. 5: AAS 74 (1982) 85-86.

[32] Cf, the formula of the Council of Trent, sess. VI, cap. 9: fides "cui non potest subesse falsum": DS 1534; cf. St. Thomas Aquinas, *Summa Theologiae*, II-II, q. 1, a. 3, ad 3: "Possibile est enim hominem fidelem ex coniectura humana falsum aliquid aestimare. Sed quod ex fide falsum aestimet, hoc est impossibile."

[33] Cf. Dogmatic Constitution *Lumen Gentium*, n. 12.

[34] Cf. Dogmatic Constitution *Dei Verbum*, n. 10.

[35] Decl. *Dignitatis humanae*, nn. 9-10.

[36] Ibid. n. 1.

[37] Cf. John Paul II, Apost. Const. *Sapientia Christiana*, April 15, 1979, n. 27, 1: AAS 71 (1979) 483; *Code of Canon Law*, can. 812.

[38] Cf. Paul VI, Apost. Exhort. *Paterna cum benevolentia*, n. 4: AAS 67 (1975)15.

[39] Cf. Dogmatic Constitution *Lumen Gentium*, n. 4.

[40] Dogmatic Constitution *Lumen Gentium*, n. 1

[41] Cf. Paul VI, Apost. Exhort. *Paterna cum benevolentia*, nn. 2-3: AAS 67 (1975) 10-11.

[42] Cf. John Paul II, Post-synodal Apost. Exhort. *Christifideles laici*, nn. 32-35: AAS 81 (1989) 451-459.

[43] St. John of the Cross, *Ascent of Mount Carmel*, II, 22, 3.

Guidelines Concerning the Academic *Mandatum* in Catholic Universities

(Canon 812)

In December 2000 the NCCB Ad Hoc Committee on the *Mandatum* sent a draft copy of these guidelines to all Bishops for their use in conversations on the local level with theologians. The final draft entitled *Guidelines Concerning the Academic* Mandatum *in Catholic Universities* was discussed and accepted for publication by the general membership at its June 2001 General Meeting. The guidelines have been authorized for publication by the undersigned.

> Msgr. William P. Fay
> General Secretary
> USCCB

Preface

On November 17, 1999, the Catholic Bishops of the United States approved *The Application of Ex corde Ecclesiae for the United States*, implementing the apostolic constitution *Ex corde Ecclesiae*. This action received the *recognitio* from the Congregation for Bishops on May 3, 2000. Bishop Joseph A. Fiorenza, President of the United States Conference of Catholic Bishops (USCCB) (formerly the National Conference of Catholic Bishops [NCCB]), decreed that the *Application* would have the force of particular law for the United States on May 3, 2001.

Guidelines

Pope John Paul II's constitution *Ex corde Ecclesiae* of 1990 fostered a productive dialogue between the Bishops of the United States and the leaders of Catholic colleges and universities. It is anticipated that this recently

Guidelines Concerning the Academic Mandatum *in Catholic Universities (Canon 812)*. Washington, DC: United States Conference of Catholic Bishops, 2001.

approved *Application of Ex corde Ecclesiae for the United States* will further that conversation and build a community of trust and dialogue between Bishops and theologians. Without ongoing and respectful communication, the implementation of the *mandatum* might appear to be only a juridical constriction of the work of theologians. Both Bishops and theologians are engaged in a necessary though complementary service to the Church that requires ongoing and mutually respectful dialogue.

Article 4, 4, e, iv, of the *Application* states that "a detailed procedure will be developed outlining the process of requesting and granting (or withdrawing) the *mandatum*." These guidelines are intended to explain and serve as a resource for the conferral of the *mandatum*. Only those guidelines herein that repeat a norm of the *Application* have the force of particular law. They were accepted for distribution to the members of the USCCB on June 15, 2001, by the Conference's general membership.

1. Nature of the *mandatum*

a. The *mandatum* is fundamentally an acknowledgment by church authority that a Catholic professor of a theological discipline is teaching within the full communion of the Catholic Church (*Application*: Article 4, 4, e, i).

b. The object of the *mandatum* is the content of the professor's teaching, and thus the *mandatum* recognizes both the professor's "lawful freedom of inquiry" (*Application*: Article 2, 2) and the professor's commitment and responsibility to teach authentic Catholic doctrine and to refrain from putting forth as Catholic teaching anything contrary to the Church's magisterium (cf. *Application*: Article 4, 4, e, iii).

c. The *mandatum* should not be construed as an appointment, authorization, delegation, or approbation of one's teaching by church authorities. Theologians who have received a *mandatum* are not catechists; they teach in their own name in virtue of their baptism and their academic and professional competence, not in the name of the Bishop or of the Church's magisterium (*Application*: Article 4, 4, e, ii).

2. Who is required to have the *mandatum*?

a. All Catholics who teach theological disciplines in a Catholic university are required to have a *mandatum* (canon 812 and *Application*: Article 4, 4, e).

b. In accord with canon 812, the *mandatum* is an obligation of the professor, not of the university.

c. "Teaching" in this context signifies regular presentation (by full-time or part-time professors) of academic material in an academic institution. Occasional lectures as well as preaching and counseling are not within the meaning of the *Application* and these guidelines.

d. "Theological disciplines" in this context signifies Sacred Scripture, dogmatic theology, moral theology, pastoral theology, canon law, liturgy, and church history (cf. canon 252).

e. "University" in this context signifies not only institutions that bear the title "university" but also Catholic colleges and other institutions of higher learning.

3. Who is to grant the *mandatum*?

a. The *mandatum* is to be granted by the diocesan Bishop of the diocese in which the Catholic university is located, generally understood to be where the president and central administration offices are located (cf. *Application*: Article 4, 4, e , iv, [1]).

b. The competent ecclesiastical authority may grant the *mandatum* personally or through a delegate (*Application*: Article 4, 4, e, iv, [1]).

4. How is the *mandatum* to be granted?

a. A request for a *mandatum* by a professor of a Catholic theological discipline should be in writing and should include a declaration that the teacher will teach in full communion with the Church.

b. The ecclesiastical authority should respond in writing (*Application*: Article 4, 4, e, iv, [3]) (see Appendix for samples).

c. An ecclesiastical authority has the right to offer the *mandatum* on his own initiative (which requires an acceptance), provided that the commitment to teach in full communion with the Church is clear.

d. A professor already hired by the effective date (May 3, 2001) of the *Application* is required to obtain the *mandatum* by June 1, 2002.

   A professor hired after the effective date of the *Application* is required to obtain the *mandatum* within the academic year or within six months of the date of being hired, whichever is longer.

   If the professor does not obtain the *mandatum* within the time period given above, the competent ecclesiastical authority should notify the appropriate authority in the college or university.

e. Without prejudice to the rights of the diocesan Bishop, a *mandatum*, once granted, remains in effect wherever and as long as the professor teaches unless and until it is withdrawn by the competent ecclesiastical authority (*Application*: Article 4, 4, e, iv, [2]). Although there is no need for the *mandatum*, once granted, to be granted again by another diocesan Bishop, every diocesan Bishop has the right to require otherwise in his own diocese (*Application*: footnote 43).

   f. If the Bishop is contemplating the denial or withdrawal of the *mandatum*, he should discuss this informally with the theologian, listing the reasons and identifying the sources, and allowing the theologian to make all appropriate responses.

5. Grounds and process for withholding or withdrawing the *mandatum*

   a. If all the conditions for granting the *mandatum* are fulfilled, the professor has a right to receive it and ecclesiastical authority has an obligation in justice to grant it.

   b. Right intentions and right conduct are to be presumed until the contrary is proven. Hence the ecclesiastical authority should presume, until the contrary is proven, that those who attest that they teach in full communion with the Church actually do so.

   c. Ecclesiastical authorities who, after discussion with the professor in question, withhold or withdraw the *mandatum* must state their reasons in writing and otherwise enable the person who believes that his or her rights have been violated to seek recourse (*Application*: Article 4, 4, e, [3]; footnote 44). Such withholding or withdrawal should be based on specific and detailed evidence that the teacher does not fulfill the conditions of the *mandatum* (these guidelines: 1, b, and c, supra; *Application*: Article 4, 4, e, iii; NCCB, *Doctrinal Responsibilities: Approaches to Promoting Cooperation and Resolving Misunderstandings Between Bishops and Theologians* [Washington, D.C.: United States Catholic Conference, 1989], III, C, 4).

   d. Any negative judgment concerning an objectionable portion of a professor's work should be assessed at three levels: (1) the significance of that portion of the professor's work within the context of his or her overall theological contribution; (2) its relationship to the larger Catholic tradition; (3) its implications for the life of the Church (cf. *Doctrinal Responsibilities*, III, C, 4).

6. Appeals and resolution of disputes

   a. Because the decision to withhold or withdraw the *mandatum* touches on the rights of theologians, the general principles of canon law should be adhered to in seeking recourse and in the process of appeal.

b. In the resolution of disputes about the withholding or withdrawal of the *mandatum*, it is important for both parties to have competent canonical and theological counsel.

c. For the resolution of disputes about the withholding or withdrawal of the *mandatum*, there should be that contact between the Bishop and the professor as urged in canon 1733 § 1. The process set forth in *Doctrinal Responsibilities* should be followed. The right of all parties to good reputation must always be honored (cf. canon 220).

d. Other means for conflict resolution on the diocesan, regional, or provincial levels (not excluding local mediation procedures) can also be invoked (cf. canon 1733).

e. While the use of informal procedures is preferable, the aggrieved party always has the right to formal recourse against the denial or withdrawal of a *mandatum* in accordance with the canonical norms for "Recourse Against Administrative Decrees" (canons 1732-1739).

7. Diocesan Bishops who have Catholic colleges or universities in their dioceses are encouraged to be available to meet with professors of Catholic theological disciplines to review concrete procedures for the granting, withholding, or withdrawal of the *mandatum* and to discuss other matters of common interest.

8. The members of the USCCB Committee for Bishops and Catholic Colleges and University Presidents and its staff will serve as resource personnel for information and guidance on matters connected with the *mandatum*.

9. These guidelines are to be reviewed after five years by a committee appointed by the Conference President.

APPENDIX: Sample *Mandatum* Draft

ATTESTATION OF THE PROFESSOR OF CATHOLIC THEOLOGICAL DISCIPLINES

I hereby declare my role and responsibility as a professor of a Catholic theological discipline within the full communion of the Church.

As a professor of a Catholic theological discipline, therefore, I am committed to teach authentic Catholic doctrine and to refrain from putting forth as Catholic teaching anything contrary to the Church's magisterium.

Signature: _____

Date: _____

Place: _____

ACKNOWLEDGMENT OF DIOCESAN BISHOP

I hereby acknowledge your declaration to remain within the full communion of the Catholic Church in fulfillment of your role and responsibility as a professor of Catholic theological disciplines.

I recognize your commitment as a professor of Catholic theological disciplines to teach authentic Catholic doctrine and to refrain from putting forth as Catholic teaching anything contrary to the Church's magisterium.

While the *mandatum* does not constitute you as an agent of the magisterium, it does affirm that your work as a professor of Catholic theological disciplines is an important part of the Church's mission.

This *mandatum* remains in effect as long as you are engaged in the teaching of theology or until it is withdrawn by competent ecclesiastical authority for a just cause.

Signature: _____

Date: _____

Place: _____

Sample *Mandatum* Draft Offered by the Bishop on His Own Initiative

MEMORANDUM
TO: Professor Thomas Bellarmine
FROM: Most Reverend Angelo Buonpastore
RE: *MANDATUM*
DATE:

This memorandum constitutes the *mandatum* that you are required to have in order to be in compliance with canon 812. The purpose of the *mandatum* is to recognize the mutual ecclesial relationship that exists between the Church and Catholic professors of theology. It also constitutes my grateful response to your participation in the Church's mission.

I hereby acknowledge your role and responsibility as a professor of Catholic theology within the full communion of the Catholic Church.

As a professor of Catholic theology you are committed to teach authentic Catholic doctrine and to refrain from putting forth as Catholic teaching anything contrary to the Church's magisterium.

While this *mandatum* does not constitute you as an agent of the magisterium, it does affirm that your work as a professor of theology is an important part of the Church's mission.

This *mandatum* remains in effect as long as you are engaged in the teaching of Catholic theology or until it is withdrawn by appropriate authority for a just cause.

This *mandatum* takes effect upon my receipt of the enclosed statement of your understanding and acceptance of its terms.

ACKNOWLEDGMENT

I, **Thomas Bellarmine,** have reviewed the *mandatum* conferred on me by Bishop Angelo Buonpastore and, by means of my signature, express my understanding and acceptance of its terms.

Signature: _____

Date: _____

Place: _____

Resource Companion

This protocol was developed by USCCB staff in consultation with the Ad Hoc Committee on the Mandatum *to assist diocesan bishops, Catholic professors of Catholic theological disciplines, and presidents of Catholic colleges and universities in the implementation of the* Guidelines Concerning the Academic Mandatum in Catholic Universities. *This protocol was not subject to a vote by the bishops.*

Professors of Catholic Theological Disciplines and the *Mandatum*

1. Catholic professor of Catholic theological disciplines requests a *mandatum*

a. The Catholic professor of Catholic theological disciplines writes to the Bishop of the diocese where the university is located (if there are branches, the diocese where the central administrative offices are located) requesting the *mandatum* and stating that s/he will teach in communion with the Church.

b. When the professor receives notification that the *mandatum* has been granted, s/he may wish to inform the chair of the Theology Department and/or the president of the university.

c. If the professor is notified that conditions for granting the *mandatum* may not be fulfilled for reasons given in writing, the professor should

(1) meet with the Bishop, if s/he has not already done so, to discuss the action, the evidence, and the reasons for the Bishop's decision, and/or

(2) be accompanied by theological and canonical counsel when meeting with the Bishop.

d. Following the meeting, the Bishop

(1) notifies the professor in writing and grants the *mandatum*, or

(2) notifies the professor in writing that he will not grant the *mandatum* giving his reasons in the written notification.

e. If the professor does not receive the mandatum, and s/he believes his or her rights have been violated, the professor has a right to

(1) seek resolution through the formal process described in *Doctrinal Responsibilities*,

(2) seek resolution through other means for conflict resolution that exist in the diocese, and/or

(3) seek formal recourse in accord with canons 1732-1739, "Recourse Against Administrative Decrees."

f. If the professor decides to seek resolution of the dispute, s/he should obtain theological and canonical counsel throughout the process.

g. If the professor decides to seek resolution of the dispute, the Bishop should participate in the process, whether the process is informal or formal.

h. The Bishop notifies the president of the college/university of the granting/denial of the *mandatum* to the professor(s) of theological disciplines.

i. Public acknowledgment of the granting, refusal by the Bishop or the professor, withdrawing of the *mandatum* for professors of Catholic theological disciplines, and responses to inquiries regarding these matters should be made in accord with a procedure worked out, with appropriate counsel, by the Bishop and college/university presidents within a diocese.

2. Catholic professor of Catholic theological disciplines receives a mandatum from the Bishop offered on his own initiative

a. The *mandatum* is offered in writing at the initiative of the diocesan Bishop. A professor receives a *mandatum* from the Bishop of the diocese in which the college/university where s/he teaches is located. The professor is asked to respond within a specified time period indicating his or her commitment to teach in communion with the Church.

b. The professor accepts the *mandatum*,

(1) acknowledges the *mandatum* in writing stating that s/he will teach in communion with the Church, and

(2) may wish to inform the president of the college/university.

c. If the professor does not wish to accept the *mandatum*, s/he

(1) notifies the Bishop in writing of the decision giving reasons for the non-acceptance, and

(2) may wish to inform the president of the college/university.

d. The Bishop notifies the president of the college/university of the acceptance/non-acceptance of the *mandatum* by the professor(s) of Catholic theological disciplines.

e. If a professor chooses not to respond to the Bishop regarding acceptance or non-acceptance of the *mandatum* within the specified time period, the Bishop may wish to notify the president of the college/university of the non-response.

f. Public acknowledgment of the granting, refusal by the Bishop or the professor, withdrawing of the *mandatum* for professors of Catholic theological disciplines, and responses to inquiries regarding these matters should be made in accord with a procedure worked out, with appropriate counsel, by the Bishop and college/university presidents within a diocese.

Diocesan Bishop and the *Mandatum*

1. Diocesan Bishop grants *mandatum* upon request from Catholic professor of Catholic theological disciplines

a. The diocesan Bishop determines whether he will delegate the authority to grant the *mandatum* and, if so, to whom.

b. The diocesan Bishop receives a request from a Catholic professor teaching a Catholic theological discipline in a Catholic college or university in his diocese for a *mandatum*.

(1) If he has delegated the authority to grant the *mandatum*, he forwards the request to the delegate.

(2) If he has reserved the authority to grant the *mandatum* to himself, he reviews the request to confirm that the professor

　i. is teaching a Catholic theological discipline, and

　ii. has stated that s/he will teach in communion with the Church.

(3) If the professor of Catholic theological disciplines teaches in a branch of the college/university located in another diocese, the Bishop may wish to consult the diocesan Bishop of the diocese in which the branch is located regarding the conditions for granting the *mandatum*.

c. If the conditions for granting the *mandatum* are fulfilled in the request,

(1) the Bishop grants the *mandatum*, and

(2) notifies the president of the college/university.

d. Public acknowledgment of the granting, refusal by the Bishop or the professor, withdrawing of the *mandatum* for professors of Catholic theological disciplines, and responses to inquiries regarding these matters should be made in accord with a procedure worked out, with appropriate counsel, by the Bishop and college/university presidents within a diocese.

2. Diocesan Bishop offers *mandatum* to Catholic professor of Catholic theological disciplines on his own initiative

a. The diocesan Bishop requests names of Catholic professors of Catholic theological disciplines teaching in Catholic colleges and universities in his diocese from the appropriate representatives of the respective institutions.

b. The diocesan Bishop determines whether he will delegate the authority to grant the *mandatum* and, if so, to whom.

c. The diocesan Bishop (or his delegate) sends a letter to each professor of Catholic theological disciplines teaching in Catholic colleges and universities in his diocese

(1) offering the *mandatum*, and

(2) requesting a response from the professor within a specified time period indicating the professor's commitment to teach in communion with the Church.

d. The Bishop receives

(1) response of acceptance from professor,

    i. acknowledges the response, and

    ii. notifies the president of the college/university.

(2) response of non-acceptance from professor,

    i. acknowledges the response, and

    ii. notifies the president of the college/university.

(3) no response from professor after specified time period has lapsed and so may wish to notify the president of the college/university of the non-response.

e. Public acknowledgment of the granting, refusal by the Bishop or the professor, withdrawing of the *mandatum* for professors of Catholic theological disciplines, and responses to inquiries regarding these matters should be made in accord with a procedure worked out, with appropriate counsel, by the Bishop and college/university presidents within a diocese.

3. Diocesan Bishop denies *mandatum* for Catholic professor of Catholic theological disciplines

   a. The diocesan Bishop determines whether he will delegate the authority to grant the *mandatum* and, if so, to whom.

   b. The diocesan Bishop receives a request from a Catholic professor teaching a Catholic theological discipline in a Catholic college or university in his diocese for a *mandatum*.

     (1) If he has delegated the authority to grant the *mandatum*, he forwards the request to the delegate.

     (2) If he has reserved the authority to grant the *mandatum* to himself, he reviews the request to confirm that the professor

       i. is teaching a Catholic theological discipline, and

       ii. has stated that s/he will teach in communion with the Church.

     (3) If the professor of Catholic theological disciplines teaches in a branch of the college/university located in another diocese, the Bishop may wish to consult the diocesan Bishop of the diocese in which the branch is located regarding the conditions for granting the *mandatum*.

   c. If the conditions for granting the *mandatum* are fulfilled in the request,

     (1) the Bishop grants the *mandatum*, and

     (2) notifies the president of the college/university.

   d. If the conditions for granting the *mandatum* do not seem to be fulfilled, the Bishop, if he judges it appropriate, asks theological and canonical counsel to review the evidence and advise him.

   e. If, after hearing counsel, the Bishop determines that the conditions for granting the *mandatum* are fulfilled, he responds to the professor in writing and grants the *mandatum*.

   f. If, after hearing counsel, the Bishop determines that the conditions for granting the *mandatum* may not be fulfilled,

     (1) he notifies the professor in writing, and

     (2) requests a meeting with the professor to discuss the evidence, stating that s/he may be accompanied by theological and canonical counsel.

   g. Following the meeting, the Bishop decides whether or not the conditions for granting the *mandatum* are fulfilled. The Bishop

(1) notifies the professor in writing and grants the *mandatum*, or

(2) notifies the professor in writing that he will not grant the *mandatum* giving his reasons in the written notification, and

(3) notifies the president of the college/university of his decision.

h. If the professor does not receive the *mandatum*, and s/he believes his or her rights have been violated, the professor has a right to

(1) seek resolution through the formal process described in *Doctrinal Responsibilities*,

(2) seek resolution through other means for conflict resolution that exist in the diocese, and/or

(3) seek formal recourse in accord with canons 1732-1739, "Recourse Against Administrative Decrees."

i. If the professor decides to seek resolution of the dispute, the Bishop should participate in the process, whether the process is informal or formal.

j. Public acknowledgment of the granting, refusal by the Bishop or the professor, withdrawing of the *mandatum* for professors of Catholic theological disciplines, and responses to inquiries regarding these matters should be made in accord with a procedure worked out, with appropriate counsel, by the Bishop and college/university presidents within a diocese.

4. Diocesan Bishop withdraws *mandatum* from Catholic professor of Catholic theological disciplines

a. The diocesan Bishop is informed in writing that a Catholic professor of Catholic theological disciplines who possesses a *mandatum* is not fulfilling the condition of the *mandatum*, that is, the Catholic professor is alleged not to be teaching in communion with the Church or to be teaching contrary to the Church's magisterium. The allegation must be written, specific as to a particular writing or public lecture, and it must detail on what grounds the teaching is not in conformity with the magisterium.

b. The diocesan Bishop

(1) reviews the allegation and the evidence,

(2) seeks theological and canonical counsel,

(3) consults other appropriate individuals, and

(4) determines whether or not the allegation is reasonable and the evidence sufficient to support the allegation.

c. If the diocesan Bishop determines that the grounds for the allegation are neither reasonable nor sufficient, he communicates this to the one(s) making the allegation.

d. If the diocesan Bishop determines the allegation is reasonable and the evidence sufficient to support the allegation, he

(1) notifies the professor of the allegation(s) and the source of the allegation(s) in writing, and

(2) requests a meeting with the professor to discuss the evidence, stating that s/he may be accompanied by theological and canonical counsel.

e. During the meeting with the professor, the diocesan Bishop, accompanied by theological and canonical counsel,

(1) presents the allegation, identifying its source,

(2) reviews the evidence alleging that the professor has violated the condition of the *mandatum*,

(3) provides opportunity for defense by the professor, and

(4) informs the professor of his or her right to seek recourse in the event that the professor believes his or her rights have been violated.

f. Following the meeting, the diocesan Bishop, after hearing from counsel, decides whether or not he will withdraw the *mandatum*.

(1) If the diocesan Bishop decides not to withdraw the *mandatum*, he

i. notifies the professor of his decision in writing,

ii. notifies the one(s) making the allegation of his decision, and

iii. may wish to notify the president of the college/ university of his decision.

(2) If the diocesan Bishop decides to withdraw the *mandatum*, he

i. notifies the professor in writing that he is withdrawing the *mandatum* giving his reasons,

ii. informs the professor of his or her right to recourse in the event that the professor believes his or her rights have been violated, and

iii. notifies the president of the college/university of his decision.

g. If the diocesan Bishop withdraws the *mandatum*, and the professor be-lieves his or her rights have been violated, the professor has a right to

(1) seek resolution through the formal process described in *Doctrinal Responsibilities*,

(2) seek resolution through other means for conflict resolution that exist in the diocese, and/or

(3) seek formal recourse in accord with canons 1732-1739, "Recourse Against Administrative Decrees."

h. If the professor decides to seek resolution of the dispute, the dioce-san Bishop should participate in the process, whether the process is informal or formal.

i. Public acknowledgment of the granting, refusal by the Bishop or the professor, withdrawing of the *mandatum* for professors of Catholic theological disciplines, and responses to inquiries regarding these matters should be made in accord with a procedure worked out, with appropriate counsel, by the Bishop and college/university presidents within a diocese.

President of Catholic College/ University and the *Mandatum*

A. Upon request of the diocesan Bishop or his delegate, the president or the appropriate representative of the Catholic college/university for-wards a list of Catholic professors of Catholic theological disciplines teaching in the college/university.

B. Following notification of the president by the diocesan Bishop or his delegate of the names of Catholic professors of Catholic theological disciplines in the college/university who have received, been denied, or explicitly or implicitly not accepted the *mandatum*, the president may wish to inform appropriate college/university personnel in accord with college/university policy.

C. Public acknowledgment of the granting, refusal by the Bishop or the professor, withdrawing of the *mandatum* for Catholic professors of theological disciplines, and responses to inquiries regarding these matters should be made in accord with a procedure worked out, with appropriate counsel, by the Bishop and college/university presidents within a diocese.

(1) Possible points to consider in developing a procedure:

    i. The *mandatum* is an acknowledgment by church authority that the professor teaches in communion with the Church.

    ii. The acknowledgment takes place in the external forum.

    iii. Neither the Bishop nor the college/university is obliged to publish a list of professors who have received *mandata*, though either may wish to do so after appropriate consultation.

    iv. In the absence of a published list, and when asked about a particular professor and the *mandatum*, the president might

        1. respond affirmatively or negatively without details,

        2. refer the inquiry to the Bishop, or

        3. respond in accord with a procedure determined in consultation with the diocesan Bishop and other appropriate persons.

    v. Reasons why a particular professor does not have a *mandatum* should not be made public without prior knowledge of the professor.

(2) The procedure should be communicated to professors of Catholic theological disciplines.

Doctrinal Responsibilities

Approaches to Promoting Cooperation and Resolving Misunderstandings Between Bishops and Theologians

June 17, 1989

Doctrinal Responsibilities initially began with the work of a joint committee composed of representatives from the Catholic Theological Society of America and the Canon Law Society of America. It was passed unanimously by both learned societies in June and October of 1983. This document was then presented to the National Conference of Catholic Bishops which remitted it to the Committee on Doctrine in the Fall of 1983. This final text was approved by the body of bishops in June 1989 as an independent document of the National Conference of Catholic Bishops and is so published.

> Reverend Robert N. Lynch
> General Secretary
> NCCB/USCC

Abbreviations

The following abbreviations are used in this document:

AAS   *Acta Apostolicae Sedis*
AG   *Ad Gentes* (Vatican II)
CD   *Christus Dominus* (Vatican II)
CLSA Canon Law Society of America
CTSA Catholic Theological Society of America
DH   *Dignitatis Humanae* (Vatican II)
DS   Denzinger-Schoenmetzer, *Enchiridion Symbolorum, Definitionum et Declarationum de Rebus Fidei et Morum*, 32 ed. (Freiburg: Herder, 1963)
DV   *Dei Verbum* (Vatican II)
GS   *Gaudium et Spes* (Vatican II)
ITC   Document of the International Theological Commission, *Theses on the Relationship between the Ecclesiastical Magisterium and Theology* (Washington, D.C.: United States Catholic Conference, 1977)
LG   *Lumen Gentium* (Vatican II)
NCCB National Conference of Catholic Bishops
PO   *Presbyterorum Ordinis* (Vatican II)

Doctrinal Responsibilities. Washington, DC: United States Conference of Catholic Bishops, 1989.

Preface

The present document constitutes a part of the continuing work by the Committee on Doctrine concerning the teaching mission of the Church. While the material was first prepared by a joint committee of the Canon Law Society of America and the Catholic Theological Society of America, with extensive consultation among bishops and scholars, this current text represents a revision drafted by the Committee on Doctrine in the winter of 1986-1987 and then emended in view of suggestions from the Administrative Committee in September 1987 and amendments or suggestions proposed before and during the general meeting of November 1987.[1] After further consultation with the full body of bishops from April through June of 1988 and with the Holy See in 1989, and subsequent revisions, *Doctrinal Responsibilities* has been clarified and strengthened as an instrument for promoting cooperation and for helping to resolve theological questions between bishops and theologians.

The document is in three parts.

I. The Context of Ecclesial Responsibilities presents a general statement of the ecclesial framework, the operative principles, and the responsibilities and rights of bishops and theologians. This section does not propose a full, much less a definitive, theological treatment. Rather it speaks in a summary and descriptive way to provide a context for the rest of the report.

II. Promoting Cooperation and Informal Dialogue recommends ways in which bishops and theologians can enhance cooperation in their common service of the gospel and the Church, especially through personal contacts and informal dialogue. This section focuses on positive efforts to promote cooperation, and also makes suggestions for actions by which bishops or theologians can screen complaints from third parties so that unnecessary disputes might be avoided.

III. A Possibility for Formal Doctrinal Dialogue sets out a suggested procedure designed specifically to deal with doctrinal disputes between bishops and theologians in dioceses. Since the circumstances in the nearly 200 dioceses of the United States vary widely, the approach given here is intended to be flexible and adaptable to local needs.

The recommended structures for promoting cooperation and for resolving doctrinal disputes draw upon experience already acquired by the Church in the United States for building a spirit of collaboration and resolving conflicts. They are designed to address the special problems of disputes of a doctrinal nature. It must be stressed that these guidelines can only serve if they are *adapted* to the particular conditions of a diocese, its history, and its special needs. The document presents a full complement of procedures as something from which bishops and theologians can draw. The adaptability of the procedures to local conditions by mutual consent of bishops and theologians should promote collaboration and conflict resolution. Although this report is concerned with theologians who are members of the Catholic Church, its approach may also prove useful with other theologians in Catholic institutions.

Both bishops and theologians are called to serve the word of God (cf. DV 10; CD 12). In the exercise of their office, bishops serve through authoritative teaching (LG 25). On the basis of scholarly competence illumined by faith (DS 3016), theologians serve through disciplined reflection seeking an understanding of the gospel for humanity today (GS 62). As they fulfill their distinctive but complementary duties, both bishops and theologians are sustained by the faith of the Church in God's revelation and by their participation in the Church's life of prayer, especially the Sacred Liturgy.

Moreover, in a time of philosophical and theological pluralism, much of which is good and enriching, the task of building cooperation between bishops and theologians becomes more urgent than ever so that Catholic doctrine may be effectively taught and intractable disputes avoided. A common commitment of bishops and theologians to the integrity of the word of God and a common sensitivity to the pastoral implications of theological teaching within the Church can make the structures suggested effective both in promoting cooperation and in resolving disputes.

The approach outlined here is offered to bishops and theologians in the United States for their use, though it does not have the status of law. Obviously, when used, these guidelines are to be interpreted in a manner consistent with the *Code of Canon Law*. Likewise they presuppose, as will be indicated in the pages that follow, the teaching of the Second Vatican Council and the subsequent statements of the magisterium on the nature of episcopal office and authority in the Church.

This document is not intended to offer suggestions for handling specific cases of dissent. Neither is it primarily to provide an approach to clarifying Catholic doctrine, although this may be one benefit of the process. Finally it does not in any way presuppose a situation of tension or envisage adversarial relations between bishops and theologians in the United States, as if the rights of one had to be protected against the other. On the contrary, the purpose of this document is to encourage increased communication and collaboration between bishops and theologians, to forestall disputes, and, if such disputes arise, to promote their resolution for the good of the faithful. Its guidelines will be reevaluated and, if necessary, refined in the light of these goals and the experience in using them.

I. The Context of Ecclesial Responsibilities

A. Context and Principles

The ecclesial context is critical for understanding the relationship between bishops and theologians, for encouraging cooperation, and for constructing an adequate approach to prevent or to address disputes related to the Church's teaching.

Before considering the different services which bishops and theologians render to the Church, it is important to recognize what they have in common as members of the Body of Christ. In virtue of their faith, baptism, and communion with the Church, bishops and theologians alike—however distinct their ministries, charisms, and authority—are dedicated to the active proclamation of the gospel and its transformative power for contemporary society. Both participate in the community's experience of faith and both seek to promote greater understanding of the word of God. In their common effort, both recognize the importance of communicating the faith with sensitivity to the cultural pluralism of today's world. Their common fidelity to the word of God permeates the particular responsibilities and rights of bishops and theologians; revelation is the good which both serve in analogous ways according to their distinctive ecclesial roles (DV 10; ITC Thesis 2). Thus, in different ways, rooted in the sacramental life of the Church, theologians and bishops discharge the mission of the Church "to show forth in the world the mystery of the Lord in a faithful though shadowed way, until at last it will be revealed in total splendor" (LG 8).

In his address to leaders of Catholic higher education at Xavier University in New Orleans on September 12, 1987, Pope John Paul II stressed this ecclesial context which bishops and theologians share in common and which helps clarify the right relations between them. These words and the practice of *communio* they embody, we make our own:

> Theology is at the service of the whole ecclesial community. The work of theology involves an interaction among the various members of the community of faith. The bishops, united with the Pope, have the mission of authentically teaching the message of Christ; as pastors they are called to sustain the unity in faith and Christian living of the entire People of God. For this they need the assistance of Catholic theologians, who perform an inestimable service to the Church. But theologians also need the charism entrusted by Christ to the bishops and, in the first place, to the Bishop of Rome. The fruits of their work, in order to

enrich the lifestream of the ecclesial community, must ultimately be tested and validated by the Magisterium. In effect, therefore, the ecclesial context of Catholic theology gives it a special character and value, even when theology exists in an academic setting.[1]

Thus, diverse gifts, ministries, and authority exist for the full development of the Church's unity in life and mission. They require an ecclesiological application of shared responsibility, legitimate diversity, and subsidiarity. Upon the bishops devolves the responsibility to encourage this diversity and to unify the various contributions of members of the Church. It is inevitable that misunderstandings about the teaching of the gospel and the ways of expressing it will arise. In such cases, informal conversation ought to be the first step towards resolution. If this proves unproductive, a reasonable, clear, and fair process must protect fundamental human and sacramental responsibilities and rights of all parties concerned. Any guidelines developed for such cases should encourage that free and responsible theological inquiry in service to the gospel which is faithful to Catholic tradition, in accord with the teaching authority of bishops, and responsive to the needs of the Church and the world. Similarly, any guidelines should promote the informed judgment of the bishops and hence their freedom to act responsibly as guardians and authoritative teachers of the faith.

Hence, the ultimate goal and importance of these procedures are to foster collaboration between bishops and theologians for the good of the entire Church, recognizing the vocation of theologians to study, clarify, and mediate the truth of the gospel which the magisterium authoritatively proposes.[2] The recommendations given in sections II and III deal with the diocese. It is advisable that attempts to resolve doctrinal disputes be made first at the local level before an appeal is made to the Holy See. Of course, any bishop or theologian can contact the Holy See directly, but in terms of subsidiarity, every effort should ordinarily be made to initiate the process within the local church.[3]

The terms *magisterium, theologian,* and *responsibilities and rights* are frequently used in this report. There is considerable variation in the current use of these words, but for the sake of clarity, the following specific meanings are stipulated here.

Magisterium will be used to refer to the ecclesiastical magisterium, i.e., to the unique teaching authority exercised in the name of Christ by the pope and other bishops united with the pope. Throughout, this document affirms the final pastoral authority of the episcopal office in the Church and the tasks of sanctifying, teaching, and ruling which are conferred by the Sacrament of

Orders (cf. LG 21; ITC Thesis 6). By their ordination and hierarchical communion, bishops are members of the college of bishops and authoritative teachers in their local churches. By virtue of their divine and ecclesial mission and with a discerning awareness of the needs of contemporary society, bishops have the pastoral duty in the name of Christ to proclaim the word of God with authority, to teach the truth of the faith, and to maintain the authentic interpretation of the word of God as it has been handed down in the course of history (cf. LG 25; DV 10). For this reason, the *Directory on the Pastoral Ministry of Bishops* stated for every bishop:

> In order that he (the bishop) may be found a faithful minister and supporter of the orthodox faith that has been handed on to him, protecting it from errors and dangers, he must diligently cultivate theological science and daily increase it with new yet proven doctrine (*Directory*, Part I, chapter 4, no. 24).

The term *theologian* in these pages is used to designate the Catholic who seeks to mediate, through the discipline of scholarship, between a living faith and the culture it is called to transform (GS 44, 62).[4] Thus, within the ecclesial community, theologians fulfill certain specific tasks. Like other Catholics, theologians live lives of faith within the community and in fidelity to the teaching authority of the Church (LG 25). Grounded in the commitment of their ecclesial faith and trained in the skills of scholarship, theologians systematically explore the nature and foundations of God's revelation and the teaching of the Church. They examine the interrelationships of Christian truths and offer interpretations of God's word in response to the challenges of contemporary society. Though theologians as such share in the Church's mission to serve the Gospel as effectively as possible and do so through their scholarly work, they are not primarily preachers or catechists. Typically, they hold a doctorate or comparable degree in one of the sacred sciences, have had extensive exposure to the Catholic tradition in their particular area of expertise, and are engaged in teaching and research in a seminary, college, or university.

The contribution and cogency of a theologian's work, therefore, depend upon scholarly competence that is rooted in faith and is faithful to the Church's teaching under the guidance of the Holy Spirit (ITC Thesis 6:2). That competence can be assessed from the quality of the evidence theologians adduce and the soundness of the arguments they advance for the sake of Christ's truth. Such competence can be shown, for example, when theologians ask searching and serious questions as they seek to discern and communicate the abiding truth of Christ. The constructive critical quality of theological scholarship does not compromise its fidelity to the Church and its magisterium, but indicates the disciplined reflection characteristic of genuine scholarly investigation.

Responsibilities and rights are used variously in law and ethics. We mean by *right* a moral or legal power to act or to be immune from injury. Responsibilities, and the rights with which they are correlative, have their source in one's human dignity, in one's standing in the Church, or from one's functions within the Catholic community. Commonly the possession of a right is distinguished from its exercise, because the exercise of a right may be circumscribed in order to protect the common good or the rights of others, even though the right itself remains intact. In the Catholic heritage, individual rights are always to be promoted within the context of the common good.[5]

B. The Responsibilities and Rights of Bishops

The guidelines proposed in this document reflect a concern to recognize and foster the responsibilities and rights of both bishops and theologians.[6]

The responsibilities and rights of bishops flow from their pastoral office of teaching, sanctifying, and governing in the Church. These tasks (*munera*) cannot be fully separated one from the other; they form a single pastoral office. Of the responsibilities and rights of bishops which arise from their pastoral task of authoritative teaching, we call attention to the following.

Preeminent among the responsibilities of bishops is preaching the word of God. Bishops are also charged to preserve and protect the truth of faith, i.e., to transmit the authentic gospel of Christ. Moreover, in the particular church where he serves, the bishop is to teach in the name of Christ and the Church; he is to make the pastoral judgment as to how the faith of the community will be publicly expressed at a given time and place. For that reason, the bishop is called upon to judge whether some opinions endanger or are contrary to faith and the Christian life. But it is also the responsibility of bishops to discharge their office so as to respect the gifts imparted by the Holy Spirit to various members of the Church. It follows that in the exercise of their pastoral role, bishops should encourage theologians to pursue a deeper understanding of the gospel and its meaning for contemporary life (LG 25; CD 12, 13, 14; PO 19; GS 62; ITC Thesis 5:1). In order to encourage theology and to make provisions for the consultation he needs in his teaching, the bishop should select the most suitable candidates for theological studies and should encourage these studies among religious communities and lay men and women within his diocese.

In addition to these responsibilities, certain rights of bishops are rooted in their task as teachers. Thus, the bishops of particular churches have the right to exercise their care for the truth of the gospel in the Church over which they preside. The bishops teach in the name of Christ and his Church, in union with the head and other members of the episcopal college. What they teach should meet with that religious reception proportionate to the degree of authority with which it is presented (LG 25; Canon 753).

But bishops also have the right to draw upon the contributions and the gifts of all who share the Church's saving mission, which includes the heralding of the faith (LG 12-13; AG 10-18). In their particular church communities bishops have the right to the cooperation and support of the priests who form one presbyterate with the bishop. Bishops also have a right to the collaboration of theologians: bishops draw on their scholarly competence and support as well as rely upon them as one necessary resource for their own ongoing theological study. Bishops consult theologians for aid in scrutinizing the signs of the time and in evaluating new issues and questions. Bishops look to theologians for aid in keeping their own formulations of Catholic belief and practice faithful to the word of God. Further, bishops have a right to require in the name of the Church that theologians faithfully discharge their own responsibility for the integrity of the gospel. Bishops must also have the freedom to teach without interference from civil authority or unwarranted criticism by theologians or others in the Church. Finally, because their solicitude extends to the universal Church, bishops have a right to expect fraternal support from one another.

C. The Responsibilities and Rights of Theologians

The responsibilities and rights of theologians may be grouped according to the ways in which theologians participate in the life of the Church.

As members of the community of faith, theologians share the common responsibility of maintaining the unity and integrity of Catholic faith, reflected in the *sensus fidei* (cf. LG 12) and the documents of tradition in which it is set forth. They must keep in mind the pastoral and missionary effects of their work (ITC Thesis 3). Theologians also acknowledge that it is the role of bishops as authoritative teachers in the Church to make pastoral judgments about the soundness of theological teaching so that the integrity of Catholic doctrine and the unity of the faith community may be preserved. In other words, theological teaching always remains subject to testing in the life of the Church and to the teaching of its bishops.

As scholars, theologians discharge their responsibility in fidelity to apostolic faith by meditative appropriation of the faith and by critical inquiry according to the principles of that branch of theology in which their work is done.[7] As they fulfill that responsibility, theological scholars must expect to exchange constructive criticism with other scholars, other Christians, and other interested persons of good will. Fidelity to the faith and to the canons of sound scholarship requires a willingness on the part of members of the theological community to exchange candid judgments on one another's work.

As members of diverse communities, theologians have the responsibility to seek suitable ways of communicating doctrine to people today. They should adapt the communication of their research to the audience of their lectures or publications, and take into account the effect their presentation may have. They should use pastoral discretion in dealing with the communications media in order to avoid any harm which might result from premature or inappropriate dissemination of their thought to the theologically untrained (ITC Thesis 3:4).

To the extent that theologians accept more specifically ecclesiastical activities, such as the formation of future priests, they must accept reasonable canonical ordering of their work.

Correlative to the responsibilities of theologians in the life of the Church are certain rights. Paramount among them is lawful freedom of inquiry and expression of scholarly opinion (Canon 218; GS 62). As they discharge their responsibilities, theologians have the right to moral support from the Church, though they must also expect and even welcome objective criticism of their work.

Closely related to that right is another: the right of the theologian to a good reputation (Canon 220; GS 26), and, if needed, the defense of that right by appropriate administrative or judicial processes within the Church. In cases of dispute, the theologian has the right to expect access to a fair process, protecting both substantive and procedural rights. In addition, as professional scholars, theologians have the right to employ the usual means of research and publication and to associate freely in private and professional groups.

II. Promoting Cooperation and Informal Dialogue

A. The Purposes and Climate of Cooperation

Authoritative teaching and theological inquiry are distinct but inseparable tasks. For this reason, bishops and theologians need to cooperate with one another in accordance with their respective responsibilities to enhance the quality of their diverse service to the Church. This cooperation is intended to realize the ideals of mutual encouragement, support, and assistance which are proposed by Vatican II, as well as to promote the efficacy of the episcopal office, the soundness of theological scholarship, and that unity without which the Church's mission in the world becomes weak and diffuse (LG 4, 13; DV 8; GS 44).

Cooperation between theologians and bishops ought to play a significant, indeed indispensable, role as context and prelude to the employment of formal doctrinal dialogue for resolving doctrinal disputes. Bishops and theologians involved in ongoing collaboration are likely to grow in respect and trust for one another and thus to assist and support their respective service to the gospel. As they appreciate each other's struggles to be faithful to the demands of the gospel according to their different functions in the Church, their mutual respect and trust should grow. This may serve to prevent theological disagreements and differences in viewpoint from degenerating to such an extent that formal doctrinal dialogue must be used to resolve the conflict.

Even in cases where formal doctrinal dialogue is employed, structured cooperation will already have established a climate in which all the parties are motivated to act prudently, patiently, and in charity (DH 14). Regular and meaningful cooperation provides the opportunity for each party to discern and clarify the responsibilities, rights, and interests of the other. Thus, if and when formal doctrinal dialogue is requested, both bishops and theologians can be aware of the necessary distinctions and of the possibilities and limitations of formal procedures used to deal with them.

Cooperation has a long history in the Church. In our own century prior to Vatican II, there were well established ways for theologians to cooperate with bishops in their tasks of teaching, sanctifying, and governing in the Church. In the 1917 *Code of Canon Law*, theologians (who were, in almost all cases, clerics) were envisaged as members of seminary faculties, as censors of books, as synodal examiners, and as conciliar and curial experts. In the revised *Code of Canon Law*, even more cooperative roles for theologians are envisaged, at least by implication.[1]

Bishops do rely upon theologians, explicitly or implicitly. Every bishop has been educated by theologians. So has every priest who cooperates with him in his ministry. Bishops have been encouraged, even charged, to study theology regularly to inform their preaching and to make their exercise of the pastoral office more effective.[2] So the appropriate questions are: How should bishops select theologians for consultation? When do they rely upon them? How is that reliance enacted?

Some bishops have appointed theologians as advisors and vicars for theological affairs, or have established boards of theological consultants.[3] The NCCB regularly calls upon theologians to cooperate in its work. While collaborative efforts like these are surely encouraging, much more needs to be done.[4]

Theologians, too, could profit from reinvigorated cooperation. Their relationship to the Church, which is an essential element in their identity and work as Catholic theologians, may take a further vital form in the course of collaboration with bishops. Cooperation would thus enable theologians better to understand and to fulfill their specific responsibilities in the Church.

While the focus of this section of the report is on structured cooperation between bishops and theologians, not all cooperation need or should take place in a formal mode. If bishops and theologians are convinced of the importance of the help they can render one another in carrying out the mission of the Church, they will be determined and creative in seeking ways to work together informally. Without the pressure of a crisis, they may find their conversations deeply nourishing and empowering. Together they need to foster regular and personal ways of contact.

The emergence of an important national issue, the promulgation of a papal document, the weeks preceding or following a meeting of the NCCB can be occasions for the bishop and theologians of a diocese to discuss materials, proposals, or concerns and to discern their local implications and applications. Further, bishops could invite Catholic faculties of theology to consider and evaluate theological issues which have arisen in the life of the Church. On the other hand, Catholic colleges, universities, and seminaries might make it a practice to invite the bishop to campus events of theological or pastoral significance. Catholic scholars at secular institutions could do the same. In some dioceses, it may be feasible for bishops and theologians to meet regularly for informal exploration of mutual concerns or simply for shared prayer.

B. Implementing Structured Cooperation

1. Suggested Areas of Implementation. Initiation and development of collaboration between bishops and theologians will not always require the establishment of new structures. Most dioceses already have offices, departments, and staffs which assist the bishop in meeting his varied and complex responsibilities. The issues and areas delegated to these offices often have important theological dimensions, e.g., health care, ecumenical relations, adult education, catechetics, liturgy, finances, and family life. It would be a relatively simple matter to invite competent theologians to serve as consultants to these offices or even as part-time staff members.

There are also other questions of concern and interest to both bishops and theologians in which a cooperative approach could yield very desirable results. The importance of these matters will motivate joint efforts to establish the appropriate collaborative structures to deal with them. Just as presbyteral councils and pastoral councils cooperate with their bishops, so ways could be developed for theologians and bishops to bring their expertise and talent to bear on concerns such as:

- the means and efficacy of the local church's proclamation of the gospel;
- diocesan goals, missions statements, and priorities;
- religious education materials in use or proposed for use in the diocese;
- health care policies and procedures;
- goals and policies of Catholic educational institutions in the diocese;
- policies and guidelines for lectures, conferences, and workshops held in the diocese;
- priorities and policies for the Church's charitable endeavors;
- continuing education for priests, religious, deacons, and catechists;
- the theological supports for diocesan statements, position papers, and testimony to be presented in various civic and legal fora;
- the theological background for pastoral letters;
- ecumenical relations;
- diocesan employment policies and procedures.

Although bishops and theologians teach in very different ways, nevertheless the position of either can become the target of complaints and charges which have no substance or merit. Although the accuser(s) might be well-intentioned, these situations are potentially volatile and enervating for everyone involved. In some dioceses, it may prove desirable to the diocesan bishop to establish a procedure which prevents groundless charges from occupying more time and attention than they deserve.

An individual or a small committee recognized by the bishop and the theological community for theological expertise, tact, and pastoral sensitivity could be appointed by the bishop to screen these complaints. All complaints about theological teaching in the diocese could be referred here, after they have been presented to the bishop as well as the theologian in question. The screening task, while respecting and protecting the dignity of the complainant, is to keep a groundless complaint from becoming a dispute which needlessly distracts the bishop and/or the theologian from their more important services to the Church.

Another area that calls for cooperation is the provision contained in Canon 812 of the revised *Code of Canon Law*. This requires theologians teaching in institutes of higher learning to have *habeant oportet* a mandate granted by the competent ecclesiastical authority. It is important that bishops and the theological community work together to formulate a constructive way of ensuring the pursuit of truth in teaching Catholic doctrine, observing church law, and respecting the legitimate concerns of the American system of higher education.

2. Means of Implementation. The first steps toward structured cooperation can be taken by the bishop or by theologians in his diocese. The bishop himself can request the theologians to provide him with the names and areas of expertise of theologians who are willing and competent to offer their services to the local church in a collaborative way. Theologians themselves could also develop such information and offer it to the bishop. Either way, the local church would have more substantial theological expertise available to it.

With a view to appointing a theological advisor, the bishop could also consult widely with theologians inside and outside the diocese. In larger dioceses, this advisor could be of great assistance for theological affairs and serve as the bishop's liaison to the theologians in the diocese. The theological advisor could facilitate contact between the bishop and the theologians. Such a person should not be the bishop's only spokesperson on theological issues, nor substitute for the personal contact of the bishop with theologians.

In large urban centers or wherever there is a sufficient number of theologians, the bishop might well consider establishing a board of theological advisors. Among other functions, the board could serve in cases of dispute as the mediating, screening, or fact-finding body, prior to the initiation of any formal procedures.

Most dioceses in the United States do not have enough theologians to implement structured cooperation very extensively on their own. While this factor presents particular difficulties, it also provides the bishops and theologians of a province or region an opportunity to realize the vision of mutual support and cooperation among dioceses set forth by Vatican II (LG 23; CD 6, 36, 37).

The theologians and bishops of a region could come together informally in the ways suggested above. They could also consider ways in which formal and regular cooperation could be established among them. For example, some dioceses have coordinated regional resources to develop more effective tribunals. Efforts have already been made in the United States with a view to sharing the theological and canonical resources of a region. The document *On Due Process* proposed a regional pooling of resources for more effective resolution of doctrinal conflicts.[5] Some state Catholic conferences have established medical-moral commissions.

Granted that the geographical distances involved make such cooperation more difficult to develop and maintain, still the advantages to be gained far outweigh the difficulties involved. Perhaps a demonstration project in a particular region could develop guidelines to facilitate regional structures for cooperation elsewhere.

Structured cooperation between bishops and theologians should, and to some extent already does, exist on the national level.[6] Prospects for developing it further, however, deserve serious consideration.

3. Principles Regarding Theological Consultants. Most theologians hold full-time positions in colleges, universities, or seminaries. As a result, in most instances of structured cooperation their role will be consultative. This means that they will serve in a part-time capacity as consultants or advisors to bishops or to diocesan departments and staffs which assist the bishop in carrying out his service to the Church.

If this form of structured collaboration is to function effectively and to realize the purposes for which it is established, certain principles should be followed.

First, theological consultants should be persons in full accord with the faith of the universal Church and aware of the ways that faith is known and lived in the particular church which they serve as consultants. The bishop is always free to choose his own advisors, but the competence of theologians who serve in any consultative capacity should be recognized by their peers. They should be selected from as many segments as possible on the spectrum of acceptable theological opinion, so that the Church can reap the benefits of the fullest range of theological resources available on particular issues or problems.

Second, there are often advantages to making public the names of consultants and perhaps even the selection process. Unnecessary secrecy can lead to suspicion and mistrust.

Third, whenever possible, consultants should serve for a fixed term. A policy of orderly succession among consultants will foster the benefits of both continuity and freshness of perspective on the issues. It will also realize the ideal of common effort which is at the heart of authentic unity in the Church.

Fourth, everyone involved centrally or marginally in the process should remember that the theological consultant, through faithfulness to the truth of the gospel and the demands of theological science, serves not only the local bishop, but also the entire local Church. Otherwise, the complementary but distinct and irreducible roles of the bishop and the theologian may be confused and the anticipated results of real cooperation may not be fully realized.[7]

C. Cooperation as Aiding Doctrinal Dialogue

As their conversation and collaboration become more common, bishops and theologians are likely to gain a greater sense of the distinct but inseparable services they perform in the one Church through, for example, authoritative teaching and pastoral leadership (on the part of the bishops) and ethical reflection, theological education, and research (on the part of the theologians). This alone should eliminate many misunderstandings between them.[8]

Regular and active cooperation will also establish a mutual personal knowledge and trust between bishops and theologians which can lessen the occasions when formal doctrinal dialogue is required to resolve a dispute. As bishops and theologians come to know each other not merely in official roles but as faithful persons, recourse to formal procedures to resolve conflicts between them should become less and less frequent.

If formal doctrinal dialogue is necessary, however, the mutual knowledge and trust established by previous cooperation will help to ensure that it works to the benefit of everyone involved. The dispute is also less likely to become an arena for an adversary relationship between the bishop and the theologian. Mutual knowledge and trust will help to maintain the unity of love throughout the course of the procedures, when tempers may be short, sensitivities acute, and feelings high. Each will more likely be concerned to protect the other's good name and reputation and to employ the formal doctrinal dialogue so as to preserve and enhance the service each offers to the Church. Both bishops and theologians will be solicitous for the maintenance and exercise of each other's responsibilities and rights.

III. A Possibility for Formal Doctrinal Dialogue

A. Purposes of the Dialogue

Collaboration and structured cooperation help to clarify doctrinal positions. Throughout such contacts there is a presupposition of sound doctrine, a presumption which holds unless it is refuted by contrary evidence. Nevertheless, there may be differences of opinion, disagreements, or questions concerning doctrinal matters. The bishop may have already deemed it necessary to speak or act publicly in an effort to provide pastoral guidance to the faithful. If these differences or actions lead to conflict or dispute, formal doctrinal dialogue may be used, always respecting the differing roles of bishops and theologians in the Church (cf. Canons 753, 218).

Such dialogue is not a judicial or administrative proceeding (cf. ITC Theses 10, 11, 12 with commentary). Its scope is to determine the facts and their theological and pastoral implications, and thereby to resolve any misunderstandings between bishops and theologians. It would precede any judgment which the bishop as authoritative teacher might eventually feel himself obliged to make for the sake of the faith of the Church. A dialogue about doctrine would also ordinarily take place before any consideration of a possible administrative response to a doctrinal matter. This distinction between doctrinal discussion and administrative action is basic. A doctrinal dialogue does not entail new obligations for bishops in their authoritative teaching or for theologians in their scholarly reflection, but offers adaptable means for both to exercise their roles as effectively as possible. By entering such a dialogue no theologian acquires the authority of a bishop, nor is a bishop expected to be a theological scholar. Each would participate according to his or her respective role in the Church, but each also as desiring greater understanding of the question at issue. If a bishop is to make a final determination of his view of a theologian's teaching, his judgment should be well informed and reasonable. While not expected to justify his decision in the manner of a scientific theologian, he should ordinarily present reasons for his judgment. If theologians are to sustain or modify their positions, they should do so through dialogue with bishops as well as with their theological colleagues. For example, if a bishop has questioned the teaching of a theologian, the theologian might request such a dialogue. On the other hand, if a bishop is concerned about the reported opinions of a theologian, he might be the one to request the initiation of formal doctrinal dialogue. In such cases, initiation of a private formal dialogue would serve the unity of the Church far better than public disagreement.

Neither a bishop nor a theologian may be *required* to use this process, and public pressure should not be brought to bear upon their choice. If they choose to do so, the dialogue would proceed through adopting or adapting any of the procedures that follow. A formal dialogue does not imply equality of roles in the Church but a structured pattern for doctrinal discussion.

Briefly stated, the purpose of formal doctrinal dialogue is to determine the nature and gravity of the issue at dispute as well as its pastoral significance and to achieve an agreement between the parties. The process will normally involve meetings, although much can be accomplished by written statements. As a sign of unity and charity, an atmosphere of prayer should mark the dialogue in all its stages.

B. Participants

For the purpose of these guidelines, the dispute in need of resolution is presumed to be between a theologian and a bishop. The theologian or bishop who requests the use of this formal dialogue is termed the *initiating party*. The other partner who agrees to this formal dialogue is termed the *second party*. Several bishops or several theologians may be acting as initiating party or second party.

Other persons may assist the principals in the formal dialogue. These may be involved in regard to one or more of the following functions.

1. *Advice.* Advisors may assist the initiating party or the second party by their advice and counsel. Advisors are selected freely by the party whom they will be serving as advisor.

2. *Expertise.* Experts may be called upon to assist the parties in reaching mutual understanding about their respective positions, to offer an evaluation of the relationship of theological statements with Catholic tradition, and to give advice about the pastoral effect of such teaching. Experts, therefore, should be knowledgeable about the matter under discussion, should be representative of the variety of views within Catholic tradition, and should participate in the process in a manner acceptable to both parties. Normally such experts will themselves be professional theologians or persons versed in pastoral ministry. While the opinion of experts, even if unanimous, is not binding on either of the parties, it should be given serious weight in proceeding with the dialogue and should not be rejected without good reason.

3. *Facilitation.* At the request of both parties, a facilitator may assist at any of the various stages of formal dialogue. The facilitator helps the process to move forward by bringing the principals to a better understanding of what each means, by setting specific questions for them, and by providing at various stages in the dialogue *a state of the question* to clarify what points are truly at issue at that particular moment.

4. *Delegation.* Dialogue is carried out most effectively in a face-to-face exchange, through which each party comes to a more personal appreciation of the other's position. Although this is the preferred method, there may be occasions when either party considers it necessary to delegate another person to assist in the various tasks of formal doctrinal dialogue. A bishop, for example, may choose to participate directly throughout this dialogue or to have his concerns represented by a theologian. In every case, however, the final statement of agreement for each task in the formal dialogue should be signed by the principal parties themselves.

C. Procedures for Formal Doctrinal Dialogue

1. Beginning the Dialogue

Either a theologian or a bishop may request formal doctrinal dialogue. But the decision to begin such a dialogue must be freely agreed upon by both.

a. Direct contact between the two parties. The initiating party should first have approached the second party in an informal manner to determine whether the apparent dispute may be immediately resolved without formal dialogue. If formal dialogue is needed, the initiating party makes a written request to the second party to enter into formal doctrinal dialogue. The written request outlines the doctrinal points at issue, the manner in which the dispute has arisen, the attempts to resolve the issue which have already been made, the specific request to employ formal doctrinal dialogue to settle the question, and initial suggestions concerning ways to resolve the doctrinal dispute.

b. Indirectly, through a contact person. A contact person may be appointed within a diocese to process requests for the use of formal doctrinal dialogue. The contact person is appointed by the bishop and should be qualified to evaluate and process such requests, generally acceptable also to the theological community and easily available for contact.

The first function of the contact person would be to determine whether the request for formal dialogue is legitimate. If the request is judged to be inappropriate, the contact person informs the initiating party, indicating the reasons for rejecting the request. If the initiating party then resubmits the request, the contact person submits it to the second party for a response.

If the request at the outset is judged to be appropriate, it is sent to the second party for a response and the initiating party is informed immediately of the date of this action. Rejection of the request by the contact person or submission of the request to the second party for response should normally take place within one month of the receipt of the request by the contact person.

2. The Response

Acknowledgment of a request for formal dialogue ordinarily should be given in writing within two weeks of the receipt of the request, and a formal response within one month of the receipt of the request.

    a. An affirmative response to the request should include an explicit commitment to formal doctrinal dialogue, a statement of the points about which both parties seem at the outset to be in agreement, the points which seem to be in dispute, and initial suggestions concerning ways to resolve the doctrinal dispute.

    b. A negative response should explicitly refuse to make use of formal doctrinal dialogue and state the reasons for refusal.

    c. If after six weeks from the date on which the formal request was sent to the second party no response has been received by the initiating party, a second request should be sent to the second party. Failure to respond to this second request within two weeks shall be interpreted as refusal to make use of formal doctrinal dialogue.

3. Agreement on Procedure

The written request for dialogue and the response may have already clarified the disagreement and the desired goal in dialogue. Nevertheless, the next step should be a preliminary agreement on the statement of the issues, on the procedures to be followed, and on the goal to be achieved by their formal dialogue.

In determining procedures, the preliminary agreement should address matters such as the following:

    a. level of confidentiality to be respected;

    b. participation by other persons and how they are to be selected (see above, B, 1-4);

    c. record keeping and, if appropriate, transcripts;

d. time limits;

e. responsibility for expenses.

Good order requires that this preliminary agreement be in writing and signed by both parties. It can be modified at any time by their mutual consent.

4. The Dialogue

Disputes between theologians and members of the ecclesiastical magisterium are usually complex and may involve deep feelings. It is not easy to decide *a priori* on the best or simplest method to resolve the situation. At the beginning it is essential that both parties be committed to the procedure. As the dialogue progresses, the parties may find it helpful to alter by mutual consent the procedures they had agreed upon.

Although disputes may be considerably different, formal doctrinal dialogue proposes primarily to clarify the objective content of what is at issue and to accomplish this through the completion of four tasks:

a. gathering data;

b. clarifying meaning;

c. determining the relationship of the points at issue to Catholic tradition;

d. identifying implications in the life of the Church.

One of the main instruments for achieving agreement is the formulation of written statements with regard to each of the tasks. These statements, signed by both parties, express points of agreement, clarify reasons for disagreement, and specify further questions to be addressed.

First Task: Gathering the Data

Since doctrinal disputes arise from public utterances or writings, the first task is to agree on what was actually said or written. There may be no disagreement as to the data at all, in which case a statement of agreement should immediately be drawn up and signed by both parties.

If the parties initially disagree about what was said or written, ways should be found to solve this difference of opinion. Examples include:

1. In written matters, copies of the actual materials should be made available to both parties.

2. In spoken matters, tape recordings, written reports, and other trustworthy records, if they exist, should be made available to both parties.

3. If no record exists, to settle the question of what was actually said or written it may be necessary to call upon witnesses.

Adequate access to the record by both parties is essential to effective dialogue. In cases in which a dispute has arisen because of complaints or accusations by other persons, the party accused or complained against has the right of access to the materials sent by the other persons—confidentiality in accord with church law, of course, always being respected. In such situations the burden of proof as to matters of fact rests on those bringing the complaint or accusation.

In determining what was said or written, it is important to specify the pertinent context, such as:

1. the literary genre: newspaper article, theological study, popular religious work, etc.;

2. the context of spoken communications: lecture, classroom, seminar, radio or television, etc.;

3. the audience addressed;

4. the level and extent of publicity.

In especially complicated matters the accomplishment of the task of gathering data may very well benefit from a facilitator who can settle factual questions to the satisfaction of both parties. The parties may also make use of advisors or, if necessary, delegates to expedite the process.

This task should be completed with a written statement of agreement, signed by both parties. It specifies the data gathered and the agreement of the parties on the essential points of what was said or written. In some cases agreement on accurate data may itself resolve the dispute and complete the dialogue.

Second Task: Clarifying the Meaning

While completion of the first task may determine clearly what was said or written, questions may still exist about the meaning of the data. Since words may admit of varying interpretations, the parties need to seek a common understanding of the meaning of what was said or written. The result of this effort should be an agreement either on a single meaning of these data or on their possible, differing interpretations.

In reaching this clarification, consideration should be given to various factors, such as:

1. the significance of the words in text and context;

2. the broader corpus of the author's work, philosophical and theological perspective, and method;

3. the author's intention in presenting the material, whether the position was being advocated, defended, described, etc.;

4. the pertinent context of the work at issue as determined in the first task (see above);

5. the degree to which the statement is presented as a personal opinion or as a teaching of the Church.

If agreement on meaning is not readily achieved, the parties may find it useful to rely on the advice of others or perhaps to submit the matter to a jointly acceptable facilitator.

This second task should be completed with a written statement of agreement, signed by both parties, expressing as clearly as possible the mutually accepted meaning of what was said or written. The statement may also specify any differing interpretations which remain. In some cases, agreement on the meaning may itself resolve the dispute and complete the dialogue.

Third Task: Determining the Relationship with Catholic Tradition

Every doctrinal dispute will initially involve at least an apparent divergence of opinion about the consonance of a public utterance or writing with Catholic tradition. The completion of the first two tasks may result in the conclusion that the disagreement was unfounded. Nevertheless, the first two tasks may simply serve to clarify the point at issue, that is, the consonance of what was said or written with Catholic tradition.

This stage of the doctrinal inquiry is complex. It is not the same as a final judgment about public teaching that the bishop may make at the end of the entire process. Nor is it a task that can be isolated from the parties themselves; their personal involvement is especially important. It is a learning process in which dialogue should assist both parties to develop a more precise understanding of the fullness of Catholic tradition. Thus, in approaching this task the parties should seek to discover points of agreement, particularly in regard to the questions which must be studied and the appropriate order for addressing those questions.

This stage of dialogue should begin with a written statement by the initiating party outlining the basis on which consonance with Catholic tradition is questioned. The second party should respond to this initial statement in writing. If no agreement is reached, these two documents form the basis for further dialogue.

The term *Catholic tradition* refers to the whole range of church teaching grounded in the word of God, especially in the Scriptures, and received in the Church through the centuries. The magisterium serves the word of God by proposing doctrine in solemn conciliar or papal pronouncements, in ordinary papal and episcopal teaching, and in other activities such as the approval of materials used in the instruction of the faithful and the worship of the Church. Catholic tradition is also reflected and furthered in the *sensus fidelium*, the works of approved authors, and in Catholic life, worship, and belief. Determining the consonance of a theological view with Catholic tradition will demand a careful consideration of the historical context and development of church teaching, an understanding of the hierarchy of truths, an evaluation of the various levels of teaching authority, appreciation of the distinction between the substance of the faith and its expression, and the degree to which the Church has committed itself in this matter.

At this stage in the dialogue the parties may be assisted by a facilitator, by personal advisors, and especially by consultation with theological experts.

This task should be completed with a written statement of agreement, signed by both parties. It specifies the steps taken to complete the task, the resulting points of agreement, and any remaining disagreement. Here, too, the written statement of agreement may suffice to resolve the dispute and complete the dialogue.

Fourth Task: Identifying the Implications for the Life of the Church

The previous tasks have resulted in agreements on the public utterances and writings in question and possibly differing interpretations and disagreements about them. The fourth task is to determine the pastoral implications of these utterances and writings in the life of the Church. While actual or apparent implications precipitate most doctrinal disputes, they are frequently the most difficult to sort out and agree upon. This task requires not merely understanding, but prudence; not just learning, but wisdom. Concern for such implications is a responsibility of both bishops and theologians.

To begin this task, the initiating party should state in writing the nature and extent of the implications. The second party should respond to this statement in writing. If no agreement has been reached, these two documents form the basis for further dialogue on this matter.

A discussion about implications cannot be simply an exchange of personal impressions. It should clarify the criteria used by the parties to assess pastoral life. Conclusions should be based on adequate information required for prudential judgments. This may necessitate gathering additional evidence. The discussion might be assisted by the opinion of persons noted for prudence and experience in pastoral and theological matters. The parties may rely on advisors or may mutually agree on a facilitator to assist in this task.

This task is concluded with a written statement of agreement signed by both parties, specifying the steps taken to determine the implications in the life of the Church and their mutual and individual conclusions. It may include actions agreed upon for the future. This written statement may suffice to resolve the dispute and conclude the dialogue, or even provide for continued review of the issue.

D. Possible Results of Formal Doctrinal Dialogue

Formal doctrinal dialogue may conclude in a variety of ways. It is important to identify the conclusion of the dialogue process and the outcome of the dispute itself. The degree of publicity to be given to the results of the dialogue should be carefully adapted to the particular situation. In every case, even if complete agreement has not been reached, both parties should discuss these matters so that both are aware of proposed actions.

These are some possible results of the dialogue:

1. The theological and pastoral issues may be resolved to the satisfaction of both parties at any stage in the formal dialogue.

2. At the conclusion of the formal dialogue the theological issue may be unresolved, but both parties may agree that the issue may remain so without the need for further action. Agreement to disagree may be a recognition of legitimate pluralism or of a situation in which pastoral responsibility requires no further action.

3. There may be no agreement concerning the theological and pastoral issues nor acceptance of the disagreement as a form of legitimate pluralism. In light of pastoral considerations, various responces on the doctrinal level are then possible. Such responses vary in purpose, intensity, and publicity. They will also depend on the qualification of the theological issue in question. The following are some possibilities:

   a. Call for continued critical theological study.

   b. Expand the context of the dialogue to a regional or national level.

   c. Restate in a positive fashion authoritative church teaching.

   d. Issue a doctrinal *monitum*, i.e., a clear warning of danger to the faith in what is being taught.

   e. Declare publicly the apparent error of a position.

   f. Classify certain positions as one of the following:

      1) a private position which may be presented by itself, provided it is not represented as official Catholic teaching;

2) a private opinion which, when presented, must be accompanied by other more acceptable positions;

3) unsuitable for teaching as Catholic doctrine.

g. Make an accurate presentation of views to the media.

E. Subsequent Administrative Action

The foregoing procedure has been a doctrinal dialogue. The best response to bad teaching is good teaching. A doctrinal response which convincingly expresses the authoritative teaching of the Church is, therefore, the most desirable response to a doctrinal dispute. Nonetheless, when doctrinal differences begin to affect the common good and doctrinal dialogue has failed to resolve them, administrative action on the part of bishops or canonical recourse on the part of theologians may be appropriate or even necessary. (On the limits of dialogue, cf. ITC Thesis 12 with commentary.)

Administrative procedures do not of themselves resolve doctrinal issues; they are intended primarily to address pastoral situations. The kind and degree of administrative action should be proportionate to the pastoral requirements of the common good and should be no more severe than those requirements demand.

The degree of understanding reached in the doctrinal dialogue should help all parties to appreciate their mutual concern for the good of the Church and will influence the decision about any subsequent action or recourse. In addition, the signed agreements of the formal doctrinal dialogue will provide a valuable record for subsequent action on the part of bishops or recourse on the part of theologians. Differences of responsibility and authority, of course, can become especially apparent at this point. But this should not obscure the fact that doctrinal truth is not decided or assured by juridical decisions alone. In all cases, bishops and theologians alike should recognize that administrative action is always in service to the truth of a gospel that is meant to free us to love God and one another.

Afterword

The Church's witness and mission in the world are seriously conditioned by its own internal care for truth and justice. Disputes about doctrines and the manner of their resolution seldom remain purely internal affairs. On the contrary, our understanding and practice of faith today concern Christians and non-Christians alike. Bishops and theologians should all be conscious that unavoidable publicity is a fact of modern life. They should take care that media involvement not render ineffective the opportunity and structure for cooperation and dialogue. They should be concerned to avoid scandal. The attitude of participants and atmosphere for process should blend civility and charity with restraint and, where necessary, that dimension of confidentiality conducive to trust, understanding, and, perhaps, reconciliation.

We believe that, with the guidance of the Spirit, the many different parts of the body of Christ can be knit together in justice and love and thereby become more truly themselves before God. In seeking clear and equitable ways to resolve disagreements about our faith, we recommit ourselves to being a Church that is one and open, a genuine community of grace sharing the truth freely given to it. Thus we choose again the life that has been offered to us, that there truly may be "one body and one Spirit, as you were also called to the one hope of your call; one Lord, one faith, one baptism, one God and Father of all, who is above all and through all and in all" (Eph 4:4-6).

NOTES

Preface

1. In June 1980 an Ad Hoc Committee on Cooperation between Theologians and the Church's Teaching Authority reported to the Catholic Theological Society of America and recommended that the CTSA and the Canon Law Society of America jointly form a committee "to develop a proposed set of norms to guide the resolution of difficulties which may arise between theologians and the magisterium in North America." (*Catholic Theological Society of America Proceedings*, 35 [1980] 331.) The two societies agreed and, in September 1980, they formally constituted The Joint CLSA-CTSA Committee on Cooperation between Theologians and the Ecclesiastical Magisterium.

   The committee divided its task into two phases. In the first, the members prepared six background studies and published them for scholarly discussion and criticism as *Cooperation between Theologians and the Ecclesiastical Magisterium*, edited by Leo J. O'Donovan, SJ (Washington, D.C.: CLSA, 1982). In the second phase, the committee worked to develop procedures for cooperation and circulated them for reaction from representative bishops, canonists, and theologians. Further, Bishop James R. Hoffman (Toledo), Bishop John F. Kinney (Bismarck), and Archbishop Daniel E. Pilarczyk (Cincinnati) accepted the committee's invitation to join its meetings and contribute to the formulation of its final document.

   The joint committee completed its procedural document, *Doctrinal Responsibilities*, and presented it to the annual meetings of the two societies in June and October 1983 where it received unanimous votes of approval. The societies then presented it to the NCCB, which remitted it to the Committee on Doctrine. After a preliminary review by the committee under the chairmanship of Archbishop John R. Quinn, *Doctrinal Responsibilities* was taken up again in 1986 by the reorganized Committee on Doctrine chaired by Bishop Raymond W. Lessard. This committee accepted the document as a working draft and collaborated with representatives of the Joint CLSA/CTSA Committee to develop it in its present form.

   Previous to this entire project, the National Conference of Catholic Bishops had adopted two other procedural documents. In 1972, the conference adopted *On Due Process*, (rev. ed., Washington, D.C.: NCCB, 1972) as a model for due process in dioceses. In 1979, the conference issued its procedures for conciliation and arbitration, *Committee on Conciliation and Arbitration*, (Washington, D.C.: NCCB, 1979). However, in contrast with *Doctrinal Responsibilities*, those procedures dealt only with administrative conflicts.

I. The Context of Ecclesial Responsibilities

1. *Origins*, vol. 17, no. 16 (October 1, 1987): 270, paragraph 7.
2. Cf. International Theological Commission, *Theses on the Relationship between the Ecclesiastical Magisterium and Theology* (Washington, D.C.: USCC, 1977) Theses 2 and 4:

   Thesis 2: The element common to the tasks of both the magisterium and theologians, though it is realized in analogous and distinct fashions, is "to preserve the sacred deposit of revelation, to examine it more deeply, to explain, teach and defend it," for the service of the people of God and for the whole world's salvation. Above all, this service must defend the certainty of faith; this is a work done differently by the magisterium and by the ministry of theologians, but it is neither necessary nor possible to establish a hard and fast separation between them.

   Thesis 4: Common to both, although also different in each, is the manner, at once collegial and personal, in which the task of both the magisterium and the theologian is carried out. If the charism of infallibility is promised to "the whole body of the faithful," to the College of Bishops in communion with the Successor of Peter, and to the Supreme Pontiff himself, the head of that College, then it should be put into practice in a co-responsible, co-operative, and collegial association of the members of the magisterium and of individual theologians. And this joint effort should also be realized as much among the members of the magisterium as among the members of the theological enterprise, and also between the magisterium on the one hand and the theologians on the other. It should also preserve the personal and indispensable responsibility of individual theologians, without which the science of faith would make no progress.
3. Subsidiarity as used in this text was introduced into ecclesiology by Pius XII in his address to the newly created cardinals of February 20, 1946:

   That is why the Apostle of the Gentiles, speaking of Christians, proclaims they are no more "children tossed to and fro" by the uncertain drift in the midst of human society. Our predecessor of happy memory, Pius XI, in his Encyclical Quadragesimo Anno on social order, drew a practical conclusion from this thought when he announced a principle of general application, viz: that what individual human beings can do by themselves and by their own forces, should not be taken from them and assigned to the community.

   It is a principle that also holds good for smaller communities and those of lower rank in relation to those which are larger and in a position of superiority. For—as the wise Pontiff said, developing his thought—every social activity is of its nature subsidiary (subsidiaria); it must serve as a support to members of the social body and never destroy or absorb them. These are surely enlightened words, valid for social life in all its grades and also for the life of the Church without prejudice to its hierarchical structure.

   Now Venerable Brethren, over and against this doctrine and practice of the Church, place in their real significance the tendencies of imperialism. (AAS 38 [1946], pp. 144-5).

   In his letter to the presidents of the Episcopal conferences throughout the world, Francis Cardinal Seper, Prefect of the Sacred Congregation for the Doctrine of the Faith, used this same principle in his formulation of the mandate for the recently established doctrinal commissions of these conferences. His Eminence connects this principle with the mind of the Second Vatican Council:

   Episcopi opera Commissionis doctrinalis uti possunt in quaestionibus quae territorium Conferentiae seu Coetus Episcopalis tangent. Ad determinandum vero quaenam negotia ad hanc Sacram Congregationem mittenda sint, prae oculis habeatur "principium subsidiarietatis," ad mentem Concilii Oecumenici Vaticani II, ita nimirum ut ordinarie ipsae Conferentiae seu ipsi Coetus per se expedient ea quae suos territoriales limites non excedunt, neque ob aliam rationem peculiarem Sanctae Sedis interventum requirere videantur (July 10, 1968, Prot. N. 214/67).

   Also see Thesis 12 in ITC.
4. From another point of view and concerned more with theology's function ad intra, the International Theological Commission recalls the assertion of Pope Paul VI and speaks of the theolo-

gians as "in some way mediat(ing) between the magisterium and the People of God." Thesis 5, n. 2. This thesis also recalls the urgent question of culture addressed in GS 62.

5. The term *interests* sometimes occurs in discussions of responsibilities and rights. In such cases, it designates other and more elusive factors in a conflict situation. *Interests* relate to particular and concrete concerns involved in the exercise of personal or official discretion. *Interests* arise in the pursuit of one's rights or obligations, or more generally, from the freedom appropriate to all the people of God. Within this ecclesial context, the procedures designed to resolve conflicts must determine facts, the responsibilities and rights of the parties, and the interests of the parties which are at issue.

6. Because those responsibilities and rights have been discussed elsewhere, they are recalled here only schematically to provide the general context for the sections that follow. See, for example, the articles by John P. Boyle, Robert J. Carlson, Jon Nilson, and John A. Alesandro in O'Donovan, ed., *Cooperation between Theologians and the Ecclesiastical Magisterium*.

7. International Theological Commission, p. 6:

> **Thesis 8:** The difference between the magisterium and the theologians takes on a special character when one considers the freedom proper to them and the critical function that follows from it with regard to the faithful, to the world, and even to one another.
>
> 1. By its nature and institution, the magisterium is clearly free in carrying out its task. This freedom carries with it a great responsibility. For that reason, it is often difficult, although necessary, to use it in such a way that it not appear to theologians and to others of the faithful to be arbitrary or excessive. There are some theologians who prize scientific theology too highly, not taking enough account of the fact that respect for the magisterium is one of the specific elements of the science of theology. Besides, contemporary democratic sentiments often give rise to a movement of solidarity against what the magisterium does in carrying out its task of protecting the teaching of faith and morals from any harm. Still, it is necessary, though not easy, to find always a mode of procedure which is both free and forceful, yet not arbitrary or destructive of communion in the Church.
>
> 2. To the freedom of the magisterium there corresponds in its own way the freedom that derives from the true scientific responsibility of theologians. It is not an unlimited freedom, for, besides being bound to the truth, it is also true of theology that "in the use of any freedom, the moral principle of personal and social responsibility must be observed" (DH 7). The theologians' task of interpreting the documents of the past and present magisterium, of putting them in the context of the whole of revealed truth, and of finding a better understanding of them by the use of hermeneutics, brings with it a somewhat critical function which obviously should be exercised positively rather than destructively.

II. Structuring Cooperation

1. Cf. John A. Alesandro, "The Rights and Responsibilities of Theologians: A Canonical Perspective," in O'Donovan, ed., *Cooperation between Theologians and the Ecclesiastical Magisterium*, pp. 101-102.

2. LG 25. See also Bishop John Cummins, "The Changing Relationship Between Bishops and Theologians," *Origins* 12 (June 17, 1982): 65-71, and Archbishop James Hickey, "The Bishop as Teacher," *Origins* 12 (July 29, 1982): 140-4.

3. "One method I find most helpful is to have the assistance of a personal theologian. . .We would not think of leading a diocese without someone trained in canon law. How much more then the presence of someone well trained in the authentic theology of the Church?" Hickey, pp. 141-42.

4. See Cummins, p. 69, for recent instances of cooperation between bishops and theologians; also, *Catholic Theological Society of America Proceedings* 35 (1980): 332-6.

5. *On Due Process*, p. 10.

6. Ibid.

7. See ITC, p. 17.

8. "The magisterium and theology have two different tasks to perform. That is why neither can be reduced to the other. Yet they serve the one whole. But precisely on account of this configuration they must remain in consultation with one another." John Paul II, *L'Osservatore Romano* [English], no. 50 (662), December 15, 1980, p. 17.

Profession of Faith and Oath of Fidelity

Editor's Note on the Profession of Faith and the Oath of Fidelity

Canon 833 of the *Code of Canon Law* obliges certain persons, before they undertake certain responsibilities in the Church, to make a Profession of Faith. Please see numbers 6-7 of Canon 833 on page 7, which are pertinent to Catholic higher education. The obligation to recite an Oath of Fidelity comes from a February 25, 1989 action on the part of the Congregation for the Doctrine of the Faith. The English translations for the Profession of Faith and the Oath of Fidelity were approved December 19, 1990 by the Congregation for the Doctrine of the Faith.

Profession of Faith

(Formula for making the Profession of Faith in those cases where it is required by law)

I, N., with firm faith believe and profess each and every thing that is contained in the symbol of faith, namely:

I believe in one God, the Father, the Almighty, maker of heaven and earth, of all that is seen and unseen. I believe in one Lord, Jesus Christ, the only son of God, eternally begotten of the Father, God from God, Light from Light, true God from true God, begotten, not made, one in Being with the Father. Through him all things were made. For us men and for our salvation he came down from heaven: By the power of the Holy Spirit he was born of the Virgin Mary, and became man. For our sake he was crucified under Pontius Pilate; he suffered, died, and was buried. On the third day he rose again in fulfillment of the Scriptures; he ascended into heaven and is seated at the right hand of the Father. He will come again in glory to judge the living and the dead, and his kingdom will have no end. I believe in the Holy Spirit, the Lord, the giver of life, who proceeds from the Father and the Son. With the Father and the Son he is worshipped and glorified. He has spoken through the Prophets. I believe in one, holy, catholic, and apostolic Church. I acknowledge one baptism for the forgiveness of sins. I look for the resurrection of the dead, and the life of the world to come. Amen.

With firm faith I also believe everything contained in God's word, written or handed down in tradition and proposed by the Church, whether by way of solemn judgment or through the ordinary and universal magisterium, as divinely revealed and calling for faith.

I also firmly accept and hold each and every thing that is proposed definitively by the Church regarding teaching on faith and morals.

Moreover, I adhere with religious submission of will and intellect to the teachings which either the Roman Pontiff or the college of bishops enunciate when they exercise the authentic magisterium, even if they proclaim those teachings by an act that is not definitive.

Oath of Fidelity
on Assuming an Office
to be Exercised
in the Name of the Church

(Formula to be used by the faithful
mentioned in Canon 833, nos. 5-8)

I, N., in assuming the office of _____,
promise that both in my words and in my conduct I shall always preserve communion with the Catholic Church.

I shall carry out with the greatest care and fidelity the duties
incumbent on me toward both the universal Church and the particular church in which, according to the provisions of the law, I have been
called to exercise my service.

In fulfilling the charge entrusted to me in the name of the Church,
I shall hold fast to the deposit of faith in its entirety, I shall faithfully
hand it on and explain it, and I shall avoid any teachings opposed to
that faith.

I shall follow and foster the common discipline of the whole
Church and I shall observe all ecclesiastical laws, especially those
which are contained in the *Code of Canon Law.*

In Christian obedience I shall unite myself with what is declared
by the bishops as authentic doctors and teachers of the faith or established by them as those responsible for the governance of the Church;
I shall also faithfully assist the diocesan bishops, in order that the apostolic activity exercised in the name and by mandate of the Church may
be carried out in the communion of the same Church.

So help me God, and God's holy Gospels, on which I place my hand.